Hummingbirds
and
Other Wonders

Hummingbirds
and
Other Wonders

RAMON DE LA VEGA CARBAJAL

iUniverse, Inc.
Bloomington

Hummingbirds and Other Wonders

iUniverse books may be ordered through booksellers or by contacting:

iUniverse
1663 Liberty Drive
Bloomington, IN 47403
www.iuniverse.com
1-800-Authors (1-800-288-4677)

Because of the dynamic nature of the Internet, any web addresses or links contained in this book may have changed since publication and may no longer be valid. The views expressed in this work are solely those of the author and do not necessarily reflect the views of the publisher, and the publisher hereby disclaims any responsibility for them.

Any people depicted in stock imagery provided by Thinkstock are models, and such images are being used for illustrative purposes only.
Certain stock imagery © Thinkstock.

ISBN: 978-1-4759-7406-5 (sc)
ISBN: 978-1-4759-7407-2 (ebk)

Library of Congress Control Number: 2013901870

Printed in the United States of America

iUniverse rev. date: 02/06/2013

Contents

To my mother: Josie C. Conway.
Mom, you've been supportive and loving;
even, from Heaven. Thank you for all our talks.

To the woman in my life: Vicki L. Merz.
No one else did it. When I couldn't carry the
heavy loads up the mountain side; you hurried
with yours; came back down, and carried mine too.
The best boat on the water; still needs a superior sail.

To my brother, Angel:
Angel; you have, in fact; been the angel
In my life. If I can claim that I'm strong, or even
Intelligent and responsible; it's only because I've
had the privilege of having you for a teacher.

My two sons, Ray and Keith:
Thank you for believing in me through the
soup and the sunshine.

To my daughter, Katelin Ann White:
You're never at a loss for comforting words of love
and encouragement, just when I most need it.

To my beloved sister, Sherry (Elizabeth) Conway:
You were the first to recognize that I was
born to do more than shine shoes and sell
newspapers in the street. You have been
my Inspiration, and I love you so.

My brothers, Manuel, David and Ruben:
I feel your love and I know that you're
watching me closely from Heaven; as
you did on Earth. I need your support. There
are no words, with which to thank you.
I am so fortunate; to have had you
in my life.

I believe that we're not writing enough books of poetry; least of all, by male writers. I respectfully, submit my book for your consideration and approval. I hope that our readers will enjoy; a "fire from the hip" book.

"Hummingbirds and Other Wonders", is the history of a boy born into poverty in a small, New Mexico town. Ramon De La Vega Carbajal, was born white, into a Mexican and Native American world. Growing up alone in the deserts of Grant County, New Mexico, provided Ramon with a lot of time to experience and contemplate life as it was in a world of welfare lines and hopelessness; and what he elected to do about it.

This book; is a commentary about humanity in general, and the paths we choose to trod. Most of all; it's the story of a boy who wanted to pull up society's shades and allow us to see that; no matter what your social status is; we're all the same and, are free to dream.

Hummingbirds and Other Wonders

Niagara Falls, Giza, and the Grand Canyon
Mental imagery that gently, stuns the senses
Why do we feel a need, to be close to wonders?
I think that, we all want to know our Creator

Why is a wonder different from anything else?
Everything is beautiful, if you want it to be
I venture to say; that, the unusual; is wonderful
Sailfish, excite us; wonders leave us breathless

Roses and orchids; terrestrial masterpieces
Ursa Major and Orion; celestial magnificence
The Impala, cougar and porpoise; poetry in motion
Bald eagle, nine pounds, floats like a sheet of silk

The Great Wall; millions labored; thousands died
The more than ninety pyramids in Egypt; locate them
The hanging gardens of Babylon; fact or fiction?
Victoria Falls, Zimbabwe; the smoke that thunders

Everything molded by the hand of God, is a marvel
I have long, adored and revered; the hummingbird
Colorful objects that sing in the sky; winged sirens
Kittens wrapped in yarn; are cute; but; they don't fly

Have you ever seen a helicopter on a training run?
Tons of steel and glass, and it can hover in place
A force of nature, at its most mysterious work
The chopper, can shoot away, like squeezing a grape

Hummingbirds are copters, clad in rainbow feathers
Imagine; wings that flap at fifty reps per second
Their turning power; is like nothing I've ever known
They remind me of Spitfire planes in world war two

I have the season and arrival time; set to the minute
I listen for the familiar, distant buzzing They're territorial; others with beaks;
had better scram My ruby-throated computer fans; show off just for me

Visit any garden, or walk in a park; but bring popcorn
Be the most popular; bring a dish of red sugar- water, too

Ode to a Hummingbird

It's not the size, of a butterfly
Has not, the grace of sparrows
His wings are small, but spry
His body floats like arrows

In written folklore, centuries past
The eagle's glory, was inscribed
Powerful talons; in legend cast
Few of wing; are so described

Small miracles; often go unnoticed
Therefore; for evermore, I dedicate:
"Ode to the Hummingbird"
Emperor of dawn, and evening late

Hypnotic humming; guitars strumming
We should have eulogized them
I hear the Queen's Guard drumming
I saw it all, in a dream, I dreamt

You pirouette, and twirl in our senses
Your beak of ebony; opens Peter's Gates
How we love, angelic dances
Sway, as a cherry leaf; your subject; awaits

Fruits of Eden's garden; are yours to keep
Savor peaches, nectarines and golden pears
Your very shadow; warms the ocean deep
Relieve us, of daily, mundane cares

Hummingbirds and us; are one in the same
We're born to love nature, and to wonder
The reality of life; is a silly game
Why we are here; is a notion we all ponder

Small things govern our simple lives
Where would we be, without the aspirin?
Bees, bring us syrup from gummy hives
Kittens, show they're, by purring

Books ofbirdsillustrated through the ages
It's sad, to discover how little we know
Color sketches of exotic birdsfill the pages
Hummers are foundon the very last row

Mickey Rooney was small; but famous
Shirley Temple, was barely three feet tall
Tiny snowflakes in December thrill us
Tiny flyers; aren't bothered by size, at all

Few can identify our small copters
We're stuck in sports and Hollywood
We're wasting awayask the doctors
You and I would fly South, ifwe could

Don't let the big things get in the way
Shiny, little wingsare gifts to all of us
I could visit an aviary, every day
Go on foot, on a bikeor take a bus

What a fuss!!
You can barely see the little guys!

My Friends, the Desert and the Sea

Steamships and tugboats with sore throats, in agony;
    Announcing passage
Aged pilots and overstretched, bearded ropes, knotted
    Onto overworked and rusting steam whistles
A strong pull, frees a long imprisoned belch;
    a long and weary cry into the night
How my sole shutters and makes me cry, in the cold
    And lonely breast of the misty, seaport town, of
    Portsmouth, New Hampshire
I hear timed bursts of sound, reminiscent of the loon
    Then; only the sounds of silence, and the breathing
    Rhythm, of the Atlantic

That was many storms and moons ago; and I miss it so
The sea was a friend I once knew in a far- away land
This morning; I awakened to find outside my door;
    A day without music and with no kiss of salt air to
    Stir my soul and start my day

Little red tugboats; pull at the strings of my heart
They remind me of bobbing apples, at a country fair
You can spend days, lounging on the beach, near
    Irish moss and sea lettuce, while you inhale sweet,
    But, pungent Pilgrim air

A wave of rose petals and orange blossoms, tumbled
    And frolicked in the sun next to my door step,
    As a fine and subtle breeze, chased merrily

As the tide pushes it's frothy, tongue onto the shore
There's a warming urge in the far corner of my soul,
    That tells me my home of saguaros and cottonwoods,
    Is where I need to be, the day my curtain opens

How I miss my old English cottage by the sea
I ache to hear the songs of the nightingale
I hear no greetings in baritone, from my chubby, tugs
Seagulls in wing, conversing as they pass, remind me of
    Ladies in a bingo hall near a rocky shore

Deserts are seas, with waves of sand, so hot; that, one
    Can see halos ascending like the long and swimming
    Fingers, of one playing a Celtic harp

On this Sahara of endless dunes, the winds from the
Mountains sculpt magnificent works of art upon
    The sandy face of the Sonoran Desert
It resembles, the not-forgotten, ladies' rolling hairdos
    Of the thirties and forties

Although my body may be in Arizona or New Hampshire
My soul is split in two. The eastern part is nestled quite
    Toasty; in a down blanket from L. L. Bean in tiny;
    Hampton Beach, New Hampshire.
The Western part of it, is enjoying the sun
    Set on the Grand Canyon, and completely mesmerized by
    The blooming yucca, in the early spring

One who thinks, that he can foresee the future, is a; "class A Dreamer",
    and I can only hope, that my days in paradise
    Will be fulfilling, as my chilly, morning walks on the shore of
    The frigid Atlantic, and the splendor of desert walks at sunrise

I once saw a man; who's hair resemble, a gray, shiny, halo
He walked on a boarded walkway, somewhere in one of
    James A. Michener's Polynesian villages
Although, he held a cane, his walk was stooped and troublesome
He looked up long enough to display; the happiest and kindest
    Face; I have ever seen

Holding onto his left elbow, was a lady with snow-white hair, and
    Light blue eyes. The two giggled like teen-agers talking about
    Their first kiss under a grapevine in Sonoma

My, my; when you get this old, it's hard to know when you've
    Said enough, too little, or nothing at all
Guess, I've said a volume full; good-by, for now

Do Fruit Trees, Grieve?

I spent the morning, in the meadows
Resting on a maple in the shadows
I dwell there, in sunshine, and in rain
I visit my yesterday, now and again

I recall my ftrst Tarzan movie
King of the jungle; he was groovy
No yodeler can holler like Edgar's Tar
In the trees and brush; he was czar

In a scene; pirates stole a baby ape
Amidst screams; kidnappers escape
Within minutes, canvas sails billow
Tears fell on beds of sod and willow

When you lose one of your own
Life takes a melancholy tone
Everything that lives; feels pain

Life is granted for divine reason
For birth, there's a time and season
Life comes forth in a spiritual way
We don't chose the weather or the day

Think of the miracle of fruited trees
First, there's pollination from the bees
A tiny bud, born of the sun, appears
Photosynthesis for citrus, grass and peas

If I picked a few; would others, grieve?
They would cry like us; I do, believe
Everything natural is born the same
We all return from where we came

Those who live and breathe; mourn
I hear crying when I harvest corn
Apple trees bear offspring uncountable
Family picked; is insurmountable

It's plain to see, that fruit trees grieve
All here toil, and we take and give
Life is pain, jubilance and surrender
Newborn are sun rays, love and splendor

Are we the same as flowers and crickets?
We all come to serve a purpose and go
I eat honey; do bees eat biscuits?
We're more alike, than you'll ever know

If this is true, everything here is equal
All civilizations; are remarkably the same
When all is gone, there will be no sequel
Natural order, is disrupted; who's to blame?

Do fruit trees grieve?
Does the willow, really weep?
Why are we sad, when leaves turn red?
We bear fruit, we all live, and, we all grieve

Don't Play with Porcupines

I knew girls all black and brown and white
Boys came in colors too, and they were alright
Many came from money and power
Daddy built them an ivory tower

Hey, who's that girl with the skinny legs?
She needs more greasy ham and eggs
Kind of tall too, and she's homely all over
She's a rover from East Dover

Must be from the poor side of town
Check her make-up, she looks like a clown
Those shoes went out the "twist"
No way, she'll make our social list

We go too far, when we talk like this
Remember what happened to Alice?
She talked rude and mean in a crowd
Now, she doesn't talk so loud

It's easy to play when you're on a team
What happens when there's no steam?
Members drop out, one by one
Alone, each pays for what she's done

Have you ever seen a porcupine?
Playing with one, is crossing the line
Don't, ever obstruct its path
It's mood will change; do the math

Porcupines wobble when they walk
Nothing gives them grief; even a hawk
You see; we weren't made to look the same
We're nature's children with a different name

Variety gives our soup some spice
Cubes don't have to be square, to be ice
If you lick a stop sign in January,
You'll look like a lizard with lots ofworry

If you see a barrel with legs; don't pet it
Let it get too close, and you'll regret it
Things rarely look, like you want them to
If you want proof of this; visit a zoo

You don't grab, slithery things in the grass
You don't give you daddy sass
You don't play on the shore of a swamp
You don't poke beehives, in a stump

And, you sure as hell, don't play with porcupines!
They have a funny way of sticking in your minds
They aren't pretty and smooth like a beaver
If you piss one off, you'd best jump in a river

Feelings are sensitive, and react like lightning
Making friends can be pleasing or disheartening
Pick your bait well; rock salt; or Hershey
Kindness feels good; try it once, and see

New classmates need friends
They'll come to you, or run; it all depends
You know what it feels like to be a wallflower
When you're alone, a minute becomes an hour

When you 're egotistical and vain
You think you're amusing, but you're insane
Thoughtless actions tum to thorns
They pierce the flesh of he, who scorns

Be careful about what you say and do
The next victim of the quills, could be you
Stop and read the signs! Don't play with porcupines!

Pokies make poor valentines

A Crazy Wind Brought Me Home

Ten pond boats in Easter-egg colors
"Red" always won, amidst hoots and hollers
I fanned with my shirt, to make them sail
I was at pond side; rain, heat or; hail

Alabama, is God's produce heaven
Worked my John Deere from dawn, to seven
I loved the cotton fields; love incomplete
I dreamed of oceans in the Selma heat

I was confused, and my family followed suit
There was a problem, but; it had no root
Friends came to visit, and only saw half of me
My feet were in loam; my heart was at sea

My good-bye, was bitter-sweet relief
I had to be *me,* or forever live in grief
"Join the Navy", signs; made me think again
It's now or never; I can't stand in the rain

Ports of call; Malta, Spain and Greece
Lotus blossoms; some islands, were Japanese
The monsoon struck with a splendid treat
Exploding skies; where dueling gods meet

A crazy wind brought me home

Angel hair breezes, sang to me softly
Oh, I belong to the Earth, not to the sea
The compass plotted a course, dew east
Lord; I've conquered my last beast

A crazy wind, brought me home
It was no hurricane, or wayward wind

I've done two tours; I should've done one
Crashing waves aren't for everyone
I love revelry, but, I was born to farm
Rising at five, didn't cause me any harm

God! The Louisiana coast! This is where I bail!
I see a shrimp boat, the captain's by the rail
A bearded man, is waving from the bow
Salty hands, saluted; middle finger to the brow

"Sir; I need a lift, closer to home"
"Welcome aboard; you live by the sea?"
"I have cotton and wheat fields to comb"
"Set me on land; near Montgomery"

A crazy wind brought me home
Those whispering, phantom, winds
A crazy wind brought me home

Thank you, Lord
A happy, farm boy

If Not For the Leaf

The Trade Winds come and the Trade Winds go
Strong in the springtime and weak in the fall
Down kneel the corn stalks, row by row
Leaves return to Earth, one and all

Maple leaves, spiral away in a downward sway
In soft and supple peat, awaits a kiss from May
The mighty oak, our refuge from July's bite
Sanctuary for airborne friends, in the dark of night

If not for the leaf:
"Like Tea in China"; would be just a slogan
If not for the leaf:
Fields and gardens, would turn to sand
If not for the leaf:
We wouldn't rejoice in the fall's golden splendor

Persians may fly about in magic carpets
I'll cruise the Nile on reed, and palm
Give me: wreaths, bouquets, and Angel Trumpets
A banana tree leaf, to cool, and keep me calm

If not for the leaf
If not for the leaf

Breaking Bread with Strangers

I can't remember the road I was on
I was obviously, in the wrong place
Pine road sign, sticking in a lawn
It was one crazy; kite-tail chase

Joplin bound; I had a gig with a band
How I missed the turn, I'll never know
At a crossing, sat a five gallon can
It pointed north with a blue, bent arrow

A tiny red, Cyclops light, came on
The tired straight six, had overheated
I found a pumpkin patch near dawn
My ride is old, but, none can beat it

I slept, on the cold bed of my truck
It felt so good, to sleep with the stars
I hope tomorrow, brings me better luck
I need: sleep, Jim Beam and cigars

There's no way I'll start this beast
Wore the battery down, trying
I guess, I'll walk due-east
IfI'm trespassing; I'm dying

At a bend; someone's waving at me
"You sure, do look a sight, Son!"
"Where in God's Heaven, might I be?"
"You'll know, when we're all done"

I went back two hundred years in history
Pine Cabin, a well, and he carried a gun
He filled a wooden bowl, and fed me
The ham is spiced, and dried in the sun

He gave me bread, in a flowered cloth
"It'll last, if you remember to cover it"
"Eat it slow; it's no sin, to be a sloth"
"Some berry wine; try to conserve it"

"The food is fine; but, how about you?"
"Winter's coming; need to make it last"
"This pork, won't last the winter through"
"How did you survive in the past?"

"A man feeds us all, with just one loaf'
"No one here hungers for Heaven 's bread"
"See the plums and peaches, in the grove?"
"I thank God; for the people we've fed"

"We break bread; to mend a soul with it"
"We pass the cup, so lips will never dry"
"Go now; and tell others what we did"
"All, is for sharing; it's easy, ifyou try"

"The mule; will take you to your truck"
"Just tum the key; it'll start just fine"
"Don't tremble; it makes Francisco buck"
"Next time you're bye; just look for the sign"

The name ofthis village, is; Saint Francis
Saint Francis of Assisi

You need to go Home

Everybody sees your body twirl
Why are you on that corner, so late?
I know how old you are; girl!
Your ride; is at the other gate

You don't wanna learn, all they know
They're seventeen; imagine them at thirty
I see them in the graveyard, row by row
Right now, you're lost, but you aint dirty

All you 'll find is: razors, aids and blow
You need to go home, girl
The world around you, is looking dark
You can't walk no more, in the park

Trash, rats and bodies on the street
Uniforms aren't walking the beat
It has nothing to do with who you are
You can be a stat, or; you can be a star

You need to go home girl!

Smoke from guns can't hide the sky
Dreams and hope are found up high
What you can imagine; you can do
It's time to decide; it's up to you

You're using your finger for a ride
They just looking at your stride
I'll take you deep, downtown
Nobody will buy you, or cut you down

Not many walkers; get this chance
You need money; but, not like this
You can wave bye-bye from a distance
This aint something, you gonna miss

You need to go home, girl!

One life here; is all you get, but
You aint checked all the options,
yet No one's gonna make me believe
You aint smart enough to leave

This hood is filled with tears and hate
Your ride's still running; it's not too late
I know a girl who was cool in school
Someone taught you, the golden rule

Go back where you were before
Aint no P.O., knocking down your door
Set yourself fee; step over the river
When you there; you can deliver

That's where you really, belong
The life you're living is a lie
You're wearing your glasses, wrong
The hill you're climbing; is too high

You need to go home

You're not turning your back on family
Finding work, won't be a problem; you'll see
Everybody's responsible for their own lives
These streets are filled with grieving wives

The rest of us, have no choice
Walk away now; and make some noise
Don't look back, Girl! Go away, girl!
We belong here; you have your own world

One less victim of that, venom needle
No more on your back, like a gutter beetle
You have to come back to the street
Need to tell every mamma you meet

"Walk across the bridge with me;
Dance to a brand new beat"

Your new life, has just begun
Look, far away from the burning sun
There's nothing to blind you, no more
You'll feel safe, when you open the door

You never belonged to the hood
You know, you was born to be good
We all have pride and we all tried
We sinned; and too many times, we lied

Sometimes; we all float away with the tide
Slide to the east, no place here to hide
You're home
Remember the words in this poem

Its Just a Toy, Daddy

Wake up, son; up and at it!
Hop out ofthat cushy, wooly bed
Did you forget what today, is?
Aint bagging any deer, doing this

Cleaned and oiled the Winchester
Gave it a doze, of rust arrester
Make sure you do the same with yours
Son, you've done well on your chores

Dad, you know my gun aint real
Skinny squirrels, don't make a meal
This Daisy gun can't kill anything big
I feel like a clown, dancing a jig

It's just a toy, Daddy! It's just a toy!

You're still young, boy
Everyone starts out with a toy
You ancestors were expert marksmen
They started with bee-bee guns, at ten

Dad, I'm meeting the guys at the field
I wanna see the Harley, Stewart built
Can I take the Ford?
No, take the bike; it's all we can afford

Met the guys near the bleachers
Hiding smoke and suds from teachers
All we had, was one six-pack
They sent me for another rack

My father thinks I'm just a kid
He'll be sorry when he hears what I did
This pellet pistol sure looks real
Humiliation doesn't heal

It's just a toy, Daddy! It's just a toy!

Grady's store, is a block away
I gotta look cool, can't shake, can't sway
I'm walking in a manly style
The register's behind the coffee isle

My jacket opened, and everyone could see
That, I'm everything a man can be
I felt white fire in my chest
God; I just flunked another test!

Why is there smoke around his hand?
I see mist and fog around the land
I'm tired, and I have to leave now
Help me stand; I don't remember how

Fire flies all around me
I can't hear, but I can see
I felt my father's calloused hand
There's ketchup on the candy stand

Son, I didn't hear when you spoke to me
I've been blind, as a fool can be
We'll hunt again in early May
He kissed my cheek; and began to pray

Thank the stars; he can't shoot like I can
He shook you up a little; that's all
You won't be trying this again
You'll live another day; Its God's call

All I Have Left, is a Prayer

I risked everything, I had
To reach Wyoming in time
I lost everything, I had
To reach Wyoming in time

All I have left, is a prayer

She said she couldn't wait anymore
Her youth was slipping away
She doesn't feel the same as before
I had no furlough, until May

My brother, wrote me a, "watch out", letter
Marie's getting married next weekend
I wanted to go AWOL; I couldn't let her
I love her; I'm going off the deep end

Snagged me a four day pass
I was stumbling in the fog
Hopped a plane; It wasn't first class
Couldn't find the strip in the smog

Three days left before the wedding
Out of money, and breathing fast
Near Tennessee; the sun was setting
The gage is winking; I'm out of gas

All I have left; is a prayer
God, please don't let me down
All I have left; is a prayer

I see the tum for Cheyenne
Things are cooking, I'm in Wyoming
That idiot is doing a hundred and ten
Car against a tree, radiator's foaming

People stretching their necks to see
A bad situation, getting worse
Trailers from California, passing me
Followed by strobes and a hearse

No one's moving anymore
People freezing, standing by their cars
Oshkosh overalls, swinging on the door
Travelers drinking from Mason jars

Just one day, before it's over
Traffic moving like a military funeral
Forty-eight miles to Grover
No cell, I can 't even make a call

All I have left; is a prayer
I've done all I can, please help me
All I have left; is a prayer

It's ten at night; I've got to keep it tight
Bells will be ringing at noon
God, help me make it through the night
The sun will be rising soon

My eyes are playing tricks on me
Like gadgets in a magic store
I'm too wired and worn out, to see
Nothing looks the same as before

Cars wrapped in crepe paper and bows
Bouquets, pink dresses and bonnets
People at the entrance in rows
I'm dying for coffee and doughnuts

Big oak doors slowly closing
Iron bells chime in harmony
The organ player's dozing, dozing
Maids of honor; way too many

Lincoln limo with six doors
Filled with penguins, nice and tall
I know it's me, she still adores
She'll lose her slipper at the ball

All I have left, is a prayer
This can't happen, it's wrong

The inside of the church is silent
I don't hear the marching music
I'm going in, dirty and spent
Marie isn't here, is she sick?

What's taking her so long?
I hope she lives where she did before
The radio's playing our favorite song
It was set for noon; it's almost four

Parked my car next to the lilac tree
Walked around to the old porch swing
She screamed when she saw me
Her hand was bare, there was no ring

All I had left, was, a prayer
Naval ship weddings are cool and salty
All I had left, was, a prayer
In dress uniform; a wedding of royalty

Never give up; prayers are answered
I wasn't alone on my journey
All I had left, was a prayer
I'm in heaven every sunny day

All I had left, was a prayer
All I had left, was a prayer
I guess, a prayer was all I needed

L.A.'s no Place for the Amish

A horse and buggy! Is it part of a scene?
I saw them once, in a magazine
Check the traffic on Hollywood and Vine
I'd sing, "Clementine", but, I forgot a line

Sordid faces, peer from Mercedes
Horns like steamboats on the Euphrates
Pilgrims on the Rodeo side of the street
Warm smiles and waves in the L.A. heat

Linen, bluish-white bonnets
I hear Gettysburg sonnets
Black, wide-brimmed hats of felt
Happy for the life Heaven dealt

Nothing seems to stir them!
Crowded streets, fast cars and mayhem
Their horse doesn't change its speed
Why hurry the steed, what's the need?

L. A's no place for the Amish

Composed, dignified and self-assured
They have no sins to be cured
What makes them so calm and satisfied?
Read the "Book"; set the "Playboy" aside

What are they doing in Hollywood?
A sense of wonder; set the mood
Learn from them, while there's a chance
There's more to life, than drinks and dance

LA's no place for Amish
They're just fulfilling a wish
We all want to know the width of the Earth
People long to wonder since birth

Long distance drivers have their rigs
Egyptians use camels to transport figs
Egotistical stars; drive a Ferrari
Entrepreneurs and producers, eat calamari

Horses and buggies; are nostalgic
This street was graced with magic
We saw civilized people, acting civil
They don't know hatred, sin, or evil

LA's no place for Amish
Like you, they go where they wish
Do you fear robbery, at the ATM?
Crime, is unknown to most of them

All my wishes and dreams
Would be sun rays and moon beams
Ifwe would forever, abolish
Blind criticism, of the Amish

By nature, we fear all that is strange
It's an inborn, defense mechanism
In war, we fire at all that's in range
Being Amish, is not anarchism

Ignorance envelopes, like a child in a womb
Raise your curtains on the stormiest days
The silver lining, will brighten the room
We'll always find blue, behind the haze

Do you thank God, for your family?
Same blood, but completely separate
You are; whom you were meant to be
Love thy brother; the situation is desperate

I love the Amish
They brighten my day
A cornucopia of goodness in one dish
We need to embrace; we need to pray

My Cracker Jack Box

First day in school, after Christmas Vacation
Grand Central Station, never sounded louder
Comparing gifts was a rowdy, showy celebration
Some had pistols, with fake gun powder

My desk was in the back, near the coat rack
I smiled, as a helicopter whizzed by
The bell rang, and the goodies found a backpack
I went to the window, and walked away in the sky

They finally asked me, what I got for Christmas
I told them, that I had a box filled with shiny things
They weren't plastic, metal or see-through glass
It was a box of Cracker Jack, tied with strings

Same kids, same "show and tell"; year after year
Junk they got the year before, only newer
We lit two red candles; we had Christmas cheer
I got the stuff, I got the year before, only fewer

Summer break came, like a revolving Macy's door
No more bragging about pricy bikes and games
I wanted to fly like a falcon; I wanted to explore
I pretended to be Davy Crockett, and Jesse James

The toys I had, were made by hand
Except my empty Cracker Jack Box
Ihad a Caterpillar dozer, when I played in the sand
With caramel corn in it; I could lure a coyote or a fox

The best way to eat Cracker Jack; is nothing new
Careful with the cellophane; cut the lid of the box
Put the top down, and lift the bottom toward you
Squeeze the sides, with the cadence of a clock

Spheres roll out, like troopers jumping from a plane
Put the big pieces on one side of the table
The smaller pieces in a long, straight, military lane
Small against large; as in the David and Goliath fable

I spent hours, playing with the box of my nutty treat
Sitting alone, at our wobbly table; was lonely
At the desert's edge; there's no one to meet or greet
My entertainment, depended, just on me

I loved my boxes with a boy in blue, and his dog
They remind me of tin can decorations, and my mother
I was happy with my present, and she; with her peanut log
I miss my New Mexico home; as I miss, no other

Expensive gifts are fun; until new models are displayed
Fancy toys are donated to "Goodwill" every year
How would those of plenty react; if Christmas was delayed?
My little box of sweet popcorn; brought me, so much cheer!

My Kite Was Black and White

Colors; like two angels just finished a paint-ball war
My kite was black and white, like a pirate ship's sails
It was made of newspaper; that had been read before
It danced in the clouds, like a swishing, sunfish tail

The grand prize, was a dramatic, silk kite from China
Rules were: Height, control, and win any way you can
The flyers came from Texas, Maine and, North Carolina
The sky was a confetti explosion, over the Yucatan'

My uncle, "Ten Horses", and I; built my kite
The frame was made of light, flexible, mesquite bush
It was cheap, but; it was strong, light and tight One
mid-April day; it took flight on the first push

Small town celebrations are a song and a hoot!
The displays are small, creative and traditional
People in flat-bed trucks; drive by, wave and toot
The gathering is Western; the flags are international

It's an excellent market for blankets and earthen ware
Bundles of rainbow balloons ascend like smoke signals
Kites, all shapes and sizes; psychedelic tadpoles in the air
Cleanse yourselves in desert air, don't sit in the malls

If you're having a down day; you won't stay that way
Riding lessons are free! Grab those reins; Tenderfoot!
Do you like archery? Fifty feet away, is a bale of hay
You don't have to hit the hull's eye, to win some loot

From above, the fair looks like an Amish, patch quilt
We're a diversity of desert tribes; a myriad of colors
Red chili by the quart; dive in! You won't feel the guilt
Our guests are farmers, miners, merchants and scholars

The desert is sacred and alive; we'll never pave it
You need to see, "The Grant County Kite Extravaganza"
Write this mystic adventure in your diary, and save it
We have more kites, than trees in; "Bonanza"

The kids from across the Gila, sported foreign kites
They were made, in: Germany, Spain, France and Italy
A panoramic painting of; winged delights
It's an exhibition of craftsmanship, and creativity

The expensive kites, were light and spun like Saturn
My kite was lithe, agile and had good balance
One by one, they climbed in a cork-screw pattern
No kite crashed or tangled; so, we all had a chance

Third place, was a trim; green and yellow swallow tail
Second place, was a red and blue, two-stick, boxwood
First place was the "Aztec Star", a home- made kite
I accomplished much more than I thought I could

I was prepared, but I didn't think, I could compete
They handed me the trophy flyer; that same night
In the following years, the styles, were not elite
Today, I can say that on my final try; I got it right

 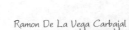

The sky's breath, can't tell luxurious from indigent
To achieve flight; learn form, weight, and the universe
Your kite should be basic, not expensive or extravagant
The winner can be, one with gold or coal in their purse

I often wonder about all the heavenly bodies around us
We, too; can fly into the dark and cold abyss of space
Remember, when the Wright Brothers were such a fuss?
You can create flight, with:paper, glue and a shoe lace

It's not winning a contest; that, one cherishes through life
In our minds will be; hilltops and the zephyr winds of March
I've shared my desert moments, with my sons and wife
It's beautiful to see your kite, waving from heaven's arch

A rainbow, feathers of the peacock and the breathing sky
The clever, study air currents and, the leap-frog seasons
Fly with a Pepsi, lightning in your heart, and a sigh
Be one with the wind; you'll feel the reasons

My kite was black and white

What's Up-You're Down

I don't see red balloons in the sky
The yard birds, aren't singing
Crows are munching on the rye
I see no robins winging

There's an evil wind a' blowing
Titan clouds are on the march
May's here, but, it's snowing
The river bed has turned to parch

What's up? You're down

You and the waves are the weather
The sun rolls up, its shades for you
You write scores with a feather
Because of you; sapphires are blue

What's up? You're down
Diamonds can wear out too
I see a child, spinning 'round
See what fame has done to you?

Take my hand and walk with me
A jewel in the raw; is just as precious
Plain or sparkling; you rival any sea
Deserts cool, when you fan your lashes

I know of a place called, Bimini
The hibiscus there, can read your mind
Nymphs from Atlantis serve you tea
Dolphins there; help you unwind

Applause, made you lose your footing
Paparazzi; stole the person that is you
Latch your door, vanity's intruding
Bathe in the Babylon, you once knew

What's up? You're down
Youth, is; but a season
Like a timepiece, it goes 'round
Innocent born; we expire for a reason

Like a rare blend of coffee, dark and rich
I will warm you, in the stormy night
Stardom unravels you, stitch by stitch, but
Sun arrows chase away the fright

Being down, is, being; half yourself
Are we, now; partially devoted to you?
The whistle's blowing; slide off your shelf
Your train is leaving; your choices are few

You have to be you

Masterpieces; are one- time miracles
Dive into the acting pool; but
You can fall offthe Earth; it's spherical
Think before you leap; you're not a fool

I Didn't Try Hard Enough

She was seen in Boston with another man
Boylston Street was plowed but, slushy
They both got a bath; courtesy of a mail van
He was embarrassed, and; she was blushing

Close to the "Bull and Finch"; they disappeared
They were last seen heading, for the cleaners
She said she met an old friend; as I had feared
They had a salad, and steamed, Vienna weiners

She's been irritable; flighty and footloose
Lately; she runs around like a cat chasing its tail
Something wasn't right; she was dropping clues
I found a receipt, from; "The Golden Quail"

It's a nice place; but It's too expensive; to go there
It's a very plush, English gourmet establishment
I asked, if she had enjoyed her meal; extraordinaire
She said it was nice, to have live entertainment

She tried to talk to me, but; I just didn't listen
I realize; there's more to being a husband, than work
Our life is good; but love and respect, are missing
I've discovered, how easy it *is*, to be a selfish jerk

I didn't try hard enough

She found her freedom, but; she's *all,* I have left
Who, did I expect her to talk *to,* when I shut her out?
I took her will to be faithful; an unforgiveable theft
I can see the hurt in her; why, won't she, just shout?

We walked for hours, and talked about her feelings
Her eyes, are filled with love, when we're together
I almost lost her; because of my wheeling and dealings
Life's too cold here; we're bound for warmer weather

I didn't try hard enough

San Diego's sunny every day, and the beaches are fine
The children are gone, but our home is full again
I've learned to work hard, but; not to *cross,* the line
There's so much; I want to say, but; how do I begin?

"I Need to Talk to you, Son"

Rusty wanted to talk to me last night
He seemed to be upset and troubled I've
never seen him so droopy and tight
Problems not aired, are problems doubled

My boy's in junior high already
He's growing up, much too fast
I heard he was going steady
Won't be his first time, won't be his last

I'm working twice the hours as before
Promotions give, and they take away
I hardly see the family anymore
You can't live both ways, they say

I need to talk to you, Son
I've been meaning to talk to you, Rusty
Mosey on over here, and sit with me
When did you get so manly and tall?
Remember how it used to be?
We played for hours, when you were small

How do I know if I'm in love, Dad?
How do I know when someone loves me?
Are these feelings good, or bad?
Love is, what love is meant to be; you'll see

Honey, Rusty has lost his shine
Walking slow, with his shoulders slumped
He doesn't act like that ole son of mine
A trip to" Burger Barn"; will get him pumped

Hey, Boss! A call for you!
"Ok, second precinct, Oakland Boulevard"
Rusty is not, a criminal; this can't be true
A thirty day restriction, to the yard!

I need to talk to you, Son
I've been meaning to talk to you

Dad, I punched a boy today
He said Lynne's been seeing other guys

She's true; I don't care what they say
I won't listen to all those lies

Why are you so quiet, Dad?
Don't you have anything to say?
Yell at me; it *won't* be so bad
Are you staying home day?

Dad; I've never seen you cry before
I tried to tell you, but, you're always tired
Son, I should cry, cry and cry, some more
I'm not a father, to be admired

There's more to being a parent, than providing
I tend to your needs, but not the most important
I should have been more available, more inviting
Wish I could start all over, but, I can't, I can't

Shame; when others know my boy better than I
I've forgotten what it's like to be young
Please forgive me, Son, I feel so bad, I could die
My new role as a real father, has just begun

I need to talk to you; Son
Problems comes up, and I forget
Things got by; that should've been done
I'll make it up to you, it's not over yet

How's Lynne Marie, doing, Son?
Let's grab a shake and talk a while

A Long and Crooked Road

Life, is like the seasons
It comes in stages, and changes course
No one knows the reasons
Birth, euphoria, ecstasy, than; remorse

My life, is a disorganized and jagged road map
I've lived in fields and, I've lived in towns
Life's road can set you free, or it can set a trap
I see phony smiles and painted frowns

It was lonely, broke, and afraid in the cities
Everything and everyone, was strange
Alleyways were filled with strolling pretties
I had hunger cramps, but I had no change

I've never been laid so low
God, please take me closer to the sea
Release me from this dungeon of sin and blow
I hurt for a place where I can be, just me

Life's a long and crooked road

There's a better life for me; that's alii know
Human nature; makes us suspicious and unkind
Point me to the theatre; I'll pick the right row
Peaceful skies and a diamond ring, haunt my mind

Some, inch ahead, while others stay behind
I pray silently, in the sting of the cold, for revival
I need a place with lemon trees; a place to unwind
When you're on the street, you live for survival

Life, is a complicated game to play
Our world, is like a carnival
Look around; you'll understand what I say
Luck in the street, brings you a curtain call

I'll stop living, if Idon't stop roaming
My bedroll and me; under sunny skies
It could be Kentucky; it might be Wyoming
I'll go South; before my dream of happiness, dies

I'll find a girl, named Katie
She'll accept and love *me*, as I am
I'll find a girl, who's a true-blue lady
I've read my last, "good-bye", telegram

This Well, Is Deep

You were sitting on the courthouse stairs
Elbows on your knees; face in your hands
Everyone saw you, but, no one cares
He was found innocent; that's how it stands

Innocent before the trial; he's the judge's son
He celebrated, while you sat in the rain
Sooner or later; we pay, for what we've done
He feels no remorse; he doesn't see the pain

This well, is deep

Every time you face a problem
Approach it like a boxing match
A smart plan can get the best of them
They won't have the time to scratch

I walked away once; but, I still love you
I'll stand with you; in the storm and sun
You told me he's a player; I already knew
Stay loose and cool; our fight has just begun

All I have is yours, and I'll give you more You
lost the first round, in kangaroo court You're
hurting; I won't leave you, like before They'll
need twice the guards around their fort

A snake isn't a rattler, if it doesn't have a rattle
Money's power; let's attack their vaulted door
A mind at peace, is a canoe and oaken paddle
A corrupted mind; just leads you to the floor

Justice will be yours, with everything it brings
They won a battle with ten; all we need; is two
The courts are for the people; not for kings
To them; truth in the court; is something new

To have a chance; we need to win the constable
Think ofthe benefits, new evidence, will reap
It's just the two of us; in this "Donner" struggle
But, this well, is deep

Lies and plastic alibis; are hard to juggle
The defense team, tosses in its sleep
Next week; they'll be reaching for the toggle
They're trapped by perjury; knee deep

Their imitation confidence, has turned to fear
His last assault; was the first rung to detention
The defense has rested; the end is near
When he gets out, he'll need old age pension

Our will to win, will never be surpassed
They can't win; purely, with "hear-say"
Today; judicial favoritism, is in the past
One more woman beater; is put away

The judges issued a hot, storm warning
Bullies look good in stripes and frowns
I hope he makes it 'til the morning
When you crop a shark's fins; it drowns

This well, is deep

I Saw a Beautiful Girl

It was the first day of sixth grade
Where will they sit me this time? T
he kids in front shine; the rest fade
I sat with the muddy boots and grime

One by one, we took our places
She arranged us like a layered cake
In the front were; all white faces
The back; dark chocolate to bake

Things didn't go as routine
She glided in about an hour later
It was a forties movie scene
Hollywood, doubtlessly made her

I saw a beautiful girl

The wind was blowing hard that day
Dust devils churning the desert sand
I had never seen nature act this way
A witch's brew on the people's land

I pulled the rope handle on our door
The smell of red chili filled the house
It was one big room, and nothing more
Mom was wearing her native blouse

She read the excitement on my face
I hugged her longer than usual
"Ma, I saw hair made of sun rays!"
"Her eyes are like a Russian jewel!"

Mamma Josie asked me ifi saw her
I had just described the girl completely
"How close were you to her?"
"As close as I could be, discretely"

Looking at someone, isn't seeing them The
outside of everything, is but a shell
Physical make up, is a dress without a hem
Look to the soul, if you want to hear a bell

I saw a beautiful girl

A perfect peach, isn't always sweet inside
We wear masks, because we fear who we are
You can touch someone, or you can hide
We often play a part to hide a scar

She's royalty and I'm a spiny cactus
We're both the same, according to the "Book"
The monsoons came, and I rode the bus
She sat next to me, and my whole world shook

I can't recall one day, when she didn't smile
"You 're quite the artist, Ray"
She spoke, and I could see the Nile
"Teach me how to draw your way"

This was my chance to search her eyes
She knew my name and I was in shock
I saw turquoise lakes and paradise
Her name was Margie McClintock

My mother was right; beauty is only skin-deep
This girl was all the wonders of the world
She's gone, but, the memories are mine to keep
I saw the beauty of all women, in just one girl

I saw a most beautiful girl

A Man in Amber

Nat Geo's latest, is about a fly in amber
Let me tell you a little story:

I was last romantic around, the fall
Common conversation, didn't flow at all
My face, then disarrayed; could stop a parade
My wife was drowning, in electric lemonade

I can't recall, ever saying; "I love you", to her
Her eyes, in vain; try to hide the hurt
The spark was fading, and we had to reignite
It had to happen soon; it had to be that night

Life was a mess; I thought my left, was right
I tried to reverse the fall, but, it was too late
When you refuse to see, you lose your sight
Did I choose this stony road, or was it fate?

We drifted apart, amidst a turbulent sky
She chose the bottle; I chose not to try
A life of work, numbs the body and soul
When ambition comes first; we lose control

I don't remember, when I was free
I lived in a bubble; designed just for me
My world, was mustard apricot in color
I yelled; but I couldn 't scream or holler

I saw bumble bees in pantyhose parachutes
There were kangaroos in army boots
They jumped off some, cherry blossoms
A girl chased, two blind, Kentucky possums

Limes and lemons racing; lemons. always win
Kindergarten kids painted me; Jell-0 yellow
I made a wobbly roulette wheel, spin, spin, spin
Fireflies near my eyes, got away; I was too slow

Did I see stretch marks on her face, last night?
No, she was young yesterday, that can't be right
Her lips were speaking; her eyes hid the meaning
I heard all that my mind wasn't screening

I live in a cellophane lily, filled with scotch
I see myself walking on Kilimanjaro's notch
My life is a menagerie, on a Barnum carousel
Reason fled some time ago; but, no one can tell

A dizzy chef, spilled yokes on my flowery walls
I'11 change it to butterscotch; before; the fall falls
The sails on my sloop; are leaves of flaming gold
I feel cold, sold, and old; if the truth be told

I'm a champagne cork, adrift on a caramel sea
My compass is gummed with guilt and misery
I can't navigate true, I need carburetor cleaner
Will this madness, change my demeanor?

Nat Geo displayed a fly, suspended in amber
I bought a copy for my barber, last December
Preserved to a, "T", in a copious drop of tea
Has the same thing happened to me?

In the winter, I feel fine; like a sparkling wine
Sweet sensations in a hot tub, that's not mine
All summer, I melt; like an icicle in a micro
To be in Tahiti; I close my eyes; and there, I go

My soul, is like blisters of fire, on the Arctic
I found the true story of me, in the attic
Familiar surname, but; not the one I carry
An inner voice; advised me; not to marry

When Sun awakens, I'll search for a sky of blue
In spring; I'll start my life anew, with you
Untrue mirror; I need a pond, to reflect me real
I see me; and I can't explain the way I feel

Dreams oftropical whimsy; play in my mind
There was thunder, and crackling, when we dined
Our first embrace, was carefully timed; and light
A subtle kiss, to seal the evening; not one, to delight

Burnt toast clouds, robust; rained new life on me
The blindness has washed away, like a rusty Model-T
I've been adrift in a boat with, Swiss-cheese sails
I'll tailor up the spinnaker, if all else fails

Oh, the Mardi Gras masks, we smith for ourselves
Tiny people accept who they are; elves are elves
Do ninety in a Porsche; and everything's a blur
Life goes by, when you too often; use the spur

The fly is a pendent, for mistaking death for honey
We choose inner darkness, when our day is sunny
We entomb ourselves, in a wad of penance
Why do we choose, the road to Pretense?

Amber, in nature; is a wonder to behold
It's a fossilized resin, produced in pines of old
Only, you; can choose the prong in the road
Only, you; can harvest the seed you sowed

See the one you love, touch the one you love
Talk to her; something she can't get enough of
If she's by your side, you won't lose your way
You're home now; make sure, that you stay

A Ride in a Bubble

We miss too much of life
Because we don't see life
We miss too much of spring;
It breezes by, too swiftly

We choose, to not stop and
Celebrate the fragrance of the
Lilacs and the cherry blossoms
Priorities are like roulette wheels

Sight, is the gift of the spectrum
With light, come the rainbows
We're privileged, to see the sunset
See Oahu in your mind, forever

Some of us possess sight, like the hawk
All of us can see our image in the eyes
Of loved ones
Some of us can see our images in ponds
And rain puddles, still rippling

Why, than; do we choose, not to see reality?
When we're needed; we look at the ground
Respond to your calling, or you may, as well
Surrender to the abyss, that is; darkness

Take a ride in a bubble

Scoot aboard; one and all!
We can't see through this human forest
It's like Fifth Avenue on a sale day
We can't navigate through our conscience
We hesitate to lift our faces, for fear, we may
See the truth and have to accept what we are

Go with me, where we can see yesterday,
Today; and tomorrow
Up, up, and; away!
This is the season of the gulf-stream
Listen to the siren, tranquilizing whispers
Of pacific and Wayward Winds

Come back from your Shangri La and
Raise the window shades

Look to the land; bear witness to your lives
There are no obstructions here
No room on board, for excuses or lies
Pure virgin air, cleanses the mind and
Extenuates the Self

You can touch eternity, here
The world below; spins like a windmill
With crushed and rusted bearings
All the easier, to see how confused we are
All; the better to see how distant we are
From the brass ring

Life doesn't just, slip by
We live life, in a tornado born of
The ten vices in stone
Birth, comes at the pace of
The Galapagos tortoise
Far too soon, and with help of
Father Time, we gather energy

We sit coiled, and waving like a flag in the
Summer breeze; to and fro, to and fro
Very much, like the cobra
When the hour glass empties;
Life springs forth with the
Velocity of the venomous serpent

Why are some able to think, in the
Throngs of this bend of time?
Life, is but a fleeting moment; very
Much like a "near-death" experience
In which we see, our life whisk by
As a quilled arrow, in flight

You be the judge
Does the thrill of fast living; enthrall you?
Do you cry in the night, because poppies
In the meadows, no longer have meaning?
The future approaches like a falling meteor

Do you foresee the end, in terror?
There are missing pieces, in your life puzzle
Look down and see; they're all around you
From this bubble, close to the Milky Way

Account for the empty moments in your life
Now; you know, where to find your future
Now you know the reality; that is you

We have to remove our physical selves
From the path of the encroaching forest
In order for the sun, to perform its magic

Come on a balloon excursion, with me
Lift your eyes, and behold all those around you
Smile, a jubilant smile, and brush away the
Smoke from your heart and from your eyes
Reach out and touch other travelers

Breathe deeply, take grip; this airship is in port
Clear your mind; chose your path; we have landed
Or, have we?

Assembly line, Henry Ford, time is precious
Machinery, car parts, and glass that shatters
Floating like a funeral procession; slow cadence
Trained hands; reach out for swinging metal

People like axels and spindles on sewing machines
Mannequins in denim, rolling conveyors, in stifled air
Laborers, standing like pylons on a Normandy shore
Clock activates an explosion of ants on the Serengeti

People in a time capsule of steel, grease, and noise
Each; emperor of a minute patch- kingdom
Jenga; make one mistake, and a world; tumbles
Assembly line reality; personifies the cruelty of truth

The Mecca Clock, ancient marvel, and Arabic pride
Behemoth factory; steel born sound, sound, sound
Locate a mouse hole, and scamper in
Beware of spinning brass, look all around

Factories, time capsules, with Achilles heals,
Blood, muscle and sinew, hand workers
Tension; resistance in tempered springs and coils
Masterfully timed, clock ballet near Mecca

Ferris wheels, shadows of man force in Michigan
Earth and pearls, spinning on a tilting axis
Factories appear and disappear as if atomized
We're spinning too fast; main cause of blindness

Gears of bronze, spinning top; time is of the essence
Time, honed to the second, product of primal need
 In a clock; intricate mechanism, bowels of a factory
No man, no industry, no industry, no man

A service for mankind, amnesty from society
It's a give and take reality
War; political disagreement, religious rebellion
Take someone's land for your own survival

Break bread, share your water, but, kneel for war
No scripture reports murder, committed for embracing
When has Jove failed to abate hatred in a savage heart
Might over weakness; who is weak and who is strong

Societies are born from mongers and steely carpet-baggers
Sky-scrapers, cable bridges and rotating colossal signs
The mechanism of the cities; is a panoramic view of a clock's
Robotic, inner-works

Crime, hate, and mans' cruelty to man
Please send me away to a better day
The weight of incivility and indifference, suffocates me
Is my sanctuary in the heart of a coo-coo clock?

Sounds of trauma, gun smoke, wailing man and beast
The sky i_ s scarlet; our ground and shirts are crimson
Mice and winged vermin; are not the scourge of Earth
See to men who shield the truth behind religion

I want to live inside a clock
I love Alpine and Westminster music

A Curious Observation

A curious observation
Women are sheer magnificence
 Thank you, for life and direction
You're the sense; in common sense

My lover's words; are without sound
An edelweiss princess, has enchanted me
Bavarian magic in my soul and all around
Is it witchcraft, or a clever Poe mystery?

I've known girls, giddy, but clever
Bronzed by nature, and I loved them
I fell to their cunning, stealthy endeavor
My favorite rose; wears a carbon gem

They came lightly, like the spring
Dancing in a whirly, tropicalbreeze
Imitating Marilyn on a swing
Bright and sultry as you please

Ladies are like rolls of Life Savers
A kaleidoscope of colors and taste
Seductively rounded, with spicy flavors
Indulge with etiquette; do not waste

What woman is now, Helen on Earth?
This would be a most curious observation
All women are pure majesty at birth
The fair sex, is the breath of a nation

Her eyes are rubies with fire, so fine
Pyramids shift, to grant her passage
Like queens; she never stands in line
She need not speak to send a message

Woman have never been, "the weaker sex"
What an interesting observation
Rarely a feminine word of glory, in any text
What an interesting observation

This world spins, because of women
What an interesting observation
A most interesting observation

Someone Took My Windmill

Hans Christian Andersen; so long ago
I snuck Indian-style, to the front of the class
Friday, was reading day, all day
I wanted White-Out opaque, on six days
The new calendar; filled with Fridays only

Ten o'clock, searing, Saturday morn
A *cocoon*, sewn from a sack of flower
Like a burrito: stuffed with one black olive
Two almonds, mint and cilantro, and an outer
Layer of pink bubble gum

One of Josie's kids, was born white, with black hair
Red, yellow and purple tulips stenciled, lightly onto a
Worn and fading, baby blanket
*Dented puzzle piece in transit; adobe walls are waiting
Earthen walls, will warm, the whitest child

A summer breeze, like a zephyr; kissed me; and, with a
Half turn; swooshed away
The desert wind, knew of my troubles, yet to come
When you drop sugar onto black sand; it shows
You're not like them, but, they want to see what you are

Mrs. Johnson; I'll remove the dusty writing all week
I'll spit- shine and buff, your, fifty-seven Bird ten times
Please slice your clock into quarters, and give one to me
A piece of an hour, would mean a life-time, don't you see?
I yearn to learn about where I was born

Barrios, in Silver City; count the ancient tribes Gila
River, serpentine, well-tempered silence Running
water, clay pipes, under-ground; North South;
sweat- dug wells through rock-hard clay Our
water's not fluoridated, but, it's always sweet

Oz tee-pee, no hides for the wind to play and sing
Jurassic giant, skeletal ribs of steel, welded tight
Monkey bars, for jubilant and playful, drifting tumblers
Magnificent silver flower in the sky, forty-eight petals
A spinning *face*, with stem that draws water from below

Steely blades, turn, stop, speed, and grind
Depending on the mood of the heavenly waves

Climate hot or artie *cold,* straight and narrow waterfall
Spills into large redwood, slatted thimbles with a handle
Windmills in Sonoran sands; windmills in wooden shoes

Forty years ago; ghosts and memories unclear in a haze
Yesteryear; pieces of mud houses, oil lamps and tin roofs
Sixty-nine, I flew east; flames like welders' torches
Hanoi, on the horizon; forth horseman firmly mounted
Cherry colored tennis balls, exploding; three-sixty

Tilt to three *o'clock,* long line of glowing stitches,
Fifteen- hundred feet below: Mekong
Four years later, Golden Gate, Dixie and Dakota heads
Falls of Niagara; half-moon rock and Booth Bay, Maine
Ulysses on terra firma, end of one odyssey

Three hours forward, Arizona time; door opens to red ants
Reminiscent, of Her Majesty's forces and American revolt
How masterfully they marched; how frequently, they fell
Arms of Thor; forward thrust; compressed steam cylinders
Arms of Zeus; pulls to free offspring of explosion

Massive serpent; with unyielding mass and symmetry
Two rails, one yard separated, dressed in armor; splintering
 Letters in Western font: Silver City, Deming and Las Cruzes
Immerge, shaking, stretching like hounds after a noon nap
Agonizing hours sardined in a rigid, humming caterpillar

On my friend; Studebaker; a peaceful, homeward slumber
No familiar sounds of iron pipes clattering near my village
Heavy wind; massive petals will, doe-zee-doe, tonight
My tin man isn't clapping, or tuning his tulip colored violin
Is my one-armed friend napping behind the cottonwoods?

Where is my house of *grass*, tin, glass and mud?
No streets with pockets full of water
They wear a shiny, black, tuxedo now
Manuel's Penny Store, is; no more for ever more
I see beehives with Match Stick People, scampering about

One mile before the last arroyo, and, no sight of my friend
No one to wave, "hello" to me; no corrugated smile for me
How, will I sooth my parched and waffling, tongue?
Stack of clay pipes, tilts towards the homes of my brothers
Have we come up, in society? Miracles sometimes happen

My spinning friend; has cycled too many Tours *D'* France
It cannot compete with the underground pipes of clay

The spit of water with the force of the Angel Falls
My stilted provider of cold libation; has melted like gold
It stood too long, and too close to the sun
Windmills; the glory of Holland
Windmills; the purpose and spirit of my soul
Windmills; ambassadors of all that represents brotherhood

Countless crisp, early fall days, I sat with my one-armed friend
We sang songs of Amsterdam and shared clear, cool water
A gift from our mother to all that breath
An oasis in America; enhanced by the presence of Dutch royalty
Windmills remain in our souls, as did, Twain and steamships

Someone took my windmill, cunningly; and, with stealth
My friend is gone, most suddenly, and; for evermore
Someone took my windmill
Willi find it, where I left my silver skates?
Lost souls, always find their way back home

*="Dented puzzle piece".
My family consisted of eight boys, no father, and my mother. I was the seventh son. I
resembled no member of my past or present family. In a Mescalero Apache family; I was
born with white skin. Damaged puzzle piece.

To Say Good-bye

"Good-bye", are the last words spoken
When; you close a door behind you
Farewells are more difficult, when a tender soul is weak
Snow on your heart; will freeze and turn to icicles
What will be your frame of spirit?

You can leave with memories of times filled with joy
Leave with a heavy heart at the helm, if you choose
It seems that in the "tender years"; life is filled with
    wishes and dreams, and at times; we're swept away with
    wild and dramatic notions of bravado

Marriage, may be swayed by harsh ocean winds, that go, not
    northward, but; are destined to take no course, at all
Make sure, that your rudder and sails are sea-worthy

Don't you know; that departure is always an inauguralstage?
It may lead to chalets amidst oak and redwood forest
    in the clouds; has begun
An adventure of a thousand miles cannot start, until a first
    step of a few inches, is initiated
Here; we bid farewell to kindred spirits, and to the valleys
    And meadows of endless skies, we have called, "home"

Time; as our youth; has come to say good-bye
The masterfully timed sting of the wasp brings instant pain,
    but; the irritation doesn't last forever
Disappointment on Valentine's Day when your favorite beau
    forgot to mark the calendar; doesn't last forever
Velvet curtains drawn at the end of "La Traviata"; bring a tear
Falling diamonds from Heaven; vanish with the warming sun
I have never known a "good-bye"; to be forever

There is always, that clinging drop of hope; that hearts still hold
    "the spark", which will once again, transform Russian winters
    to Tahitian splendor

Good-bye is not forever

You see; the future doesn't belong to us
"Good-bye", are the loneliest words we will ever cry; and
    when we speak; we must say less with our lips and
    more with our eyes and with our hearts

Separation, is another word for, "change"
No one welcomes separation from a place of comfort
Our home; is a living part of us
Destiny is preordained, and, we exist; as if by wire

What happens; when we extricate a pearl from its shell?
This precious gem of the sea; is an irritant
Ulcers will end our lives, unless we appropriate change
Natural instincts, tell us when it's time to migrate

We migrate because, too often; *we're* in the wrong shell
It's unnatural to leave your cozy, little gopher hole
When life collapses, you flee; or, you suffocate
We become attached to our environment, very much like
    seeds within a pumpkin
But, than; seeds have to be free to continue the species

Finally; there is no pain capsule; that can sooth the agony
    of saying; "good-bye"
"Good-bye"; places us in uncertainty and, *we're* all afraid
    of the unknown

Good-by, for now, and, farewell

There's Always Time for Beer

Hey Dan! I stopped by this morning
Looks like you have a junk business going
There's a note on your door, with a warning
You've been gone too long, and it's showing

Sis heated some coffee; two days old
The icebox is bare as the baby's butt
They can't shower, because the water's cold
You need to stand up; and make the cut

There's always time for boozing, Dan
You can buy a dozen eggs for the price of a beer
Your home's shutting down like; and old brass fan
Sherry cries, and I'd better not see another tear

There's always time for beer, Dan

The gang was inseparable in high school
Only six of us, but we had the coolest cars
After a beer or two, you acted like a fool
We took to growing up; you took to sleazy bars

We graduated, and the group spread out
Some married; and some joined the Marines
Sis wanted to know what you were all about
I remember the day; you exchanged rings

You hop jobs, like someone on the run
Responsibility scares you to death
You left a loving family, to have fun
I'll set you straight, if it takes my last breath

There's always time for beer

Looking cool in your Sears uniform, Dan
Service manager of auto repairs; alright!
You're standing tall; I'm looking at a man
Smiles are served at *six*, every night?

We'll never know what made you change
You must have seen the love we have for you
From partier to devoted husband; strange!
You said:barbecue Sunday, around two!

Dan, let's go have a round at "Donny Joe's"
You're cooking lasagna, tonight?
What's next? God only knows!
You're finally awake and, you're doing it right

How Dirty Is Your Clean House?

In sixty-seven, I wore a green uniform
We were drafted into the "police action"
Colleges were jammed, to weather the storm
I knew nothing about a socialist faction

Our quarterback could rifle the ball, a mile
Now, he can't even smile
Went to Vietnam, and came under attack
Now we have him, "sort of' back

In high school; you were all about him
Like a kitten begging for its milk
Chances he'd ask you out; were slim
He liked girls in velvet and silk

He's been home since June
You haven't gone to visit him
He used to gaze at the stars and moon
Now, his world's cold and dim

We saw you at the general
I was talking to Chance 'bout old friends
Saw Stuart last Sunday; at a funeral
He stood without you, by the fence

How dirty is your clean house; Mary Jane?
Some say; it's too dark in there, to tell

Everyone I see, looks the same 'ole way
You're still pretty, but something's missing
Dad said the same thing, the other day
Six years married, but, there's no kissing

The talk is; you live in a Taj Mahal It
shines like a Georgian Mansion
Crystal chandeliers give no light at all
There's no talking, you can cut the tension

How dirty, is your clean house, Mary Jane?

There are skeletons in every closet
Love letters between the mattresses
Hiding from the truth can cause it
Your bronze doors grant no access

Gossip can start like a prairie fire
You think he doesn't know, but he notices
You were wearing, racy sports attire
Spicy news; fill coffee shops and offices

Wearing shades in your lawyer's office
Doesn't fool the gossipers at all
You had it all; now, you hide your face
You're dating strangers, rich and tall

How dirty is your clean house?
Just, how dirty; is your clean house, Mary Jane?

Sing Me a New Song

My "F" one-fifty's, kicking up gravel
I'm sliding onto West Lake Road
The truck is high and level
I just dropped a heavy load

What song will she sing this time?
Sing me a new song, Terrie
Not the same note; or the same rhyme
I had a hell of a time in Tennessee

She's up town most every night
Dirty clothes, scattered all around
No call, no note; that just aint right
A neighbor said, she was city bound

Thank God for quick- frozen dinners
I hate eating alone, but the grub's good
Crap on TV: talk shows, war and sinners
She aint behaving, like a mother should

The creaky, worn out stairs, woke me up
Click; she's turning the door knob
Peas in my plate and Daniels in my cup
Told me, she's been looking for a job

Sing me a new song; a just for me, song

Memphis has the best roads in the USA
Masterpieces ofblacktop, all around us
Some take you near; some far away
I'll be on one tomorrow; in a Memphis bus

My "F" one-fifty, was kicking up gravel
I was driving on West Lake Road
Her kisses helped me to unravel
She was lonely, and; it showed

She should've sung me a new song
She should 've met me at the door
I can't see her smile, it's been too long
I miss the good times; I hurt for more

Sing me a new song
Sing me a true love song; if you will
Tell me why you did me wrong
I can't help it, ifI love you still

The memories behind the pain, still live
Hurt fades away, like an Orleans fog
All of God's sinners, must forgive
There is no direction, in this smog

I can't help it, ifI still love you
I can't help it, ifI still love you

It Doesn't Matter Who's Right or Wrong

Leaving, won't set things right
Words fade in the wind forever
Love slips away in the night
We say hurtful things to be clever

It doesn't matter who was right or wrong
It doesn't matter; yesterday's gone
Smiles were real, and hugs were expected
Surprise gifts were happily accepted

Kindness wasn't taken for granted
Our meals were poor, but home-made
I miss songbirds, and the cottage we rented
You were, "Alice", in the Disney parade

Memories; are now lifeless shadows
Our grassy path is now bramble and stones
There's an eerie stillness in the meadows
Those mounds of dust, were once pine cones

It doesn't matter who was right or wrong
We have to stop singing the same ole song
It doesn't matter who was right or wrong

If you let a fire burn too long, it's too late
Drench it, when it's a flame
The magic is gone, when you don't relate
Fires and marriages are much the same

Wise men know when to run or stand
When to fold the cards and keep their pay
When you 're beaten, extend your hand
If you're losing, Maverick; call it a day

It doesn't matter who's right or wrong
Doesn't matter; who's weak or strong
It just, doesn't matter!

You always guzzle the most beer
Reality's already set in stone
Know when to put your truck in gear
When love turns cold, you stand alone

I was at Eagle Lake, Memorial Day
The clouds were fancy-free and white
A clear mind is golden, I hear say
I still miss her in the night

God, I hope she's alright
We did everything together
I see her in the morning light
Fussing with her lilacs and heather

Do we understand our wishes?
Are we smart or just spontaneous?
Is making up, like washing dishes?
Miss Communication; please entertain us

Does it matter; who was right or wrong?
Still, destiny moves in one direction
Nothing matters, when it's said and done
You don't pass this way, without rejection

It doesn't matter, who's right or wrong

You Never Felt the Cold

Nebraska snow; was like jagged pea stone
The wind drove it like a sandblaster
Rays of ice, went through the bone
I don't know how we survived that disaster

The school bell usually rang at eight
I stood with my back to the storm
In front of the main, oak and iron gate
I was the blanket, that kept you warm

You never felt the cold

The summer, of your sixteenth birthday
Brought a change in everyone's weather
A New York family, moved here to stay
We didn't spend much time together

Your mother told me, you went somewhere
You didn't call me, and, you didn't visit
Through the screen, I saw two in one chair
Your face was close to his; I saw him kiss it

I lost my heart and soul that night
My life was: home, God, and you
He likes to play where the lights are bright
Alone now; there's nothing you can do

You never felt the cold

You were born a cuddled, prairie vixen
You wear clothes from; Fifth Avenue
There's been a wicket brew, a' mixing
Not every man; was to be a fool for you

You're the only girl in a family of six
Daddy's special, fairy tale princess
Little dreamer; reality and stories, don't mix
Affairs are fun; but, true love's priceless

I lost my heart and soul that night
My life was: home, God, and you
He likes to play where the lights are bright
Alone now; there's nothing you can do

High school was fun, but not for me
You chased the pitcher, and the quarterback
Your reputation turned hot and steamy
I saw it from the bottom of the stack

You never felt the cold

I caught a lot of colds when I was younger
The only jacket I had; I put on you
Those small sacrifices, made me stronger
I'm still standing, and, I can start anew

There's a biting chill in the air
You're cold, and nothing can warm you
Life's marching by and, you just stand there
I see icicles; that once were morning dew

I need to shield you from the wind again
We all succumb to young and wild desires
When you most needed me; I ran
God forgives us; cheaters, users and liars

There's a chill in the air
Come to me; you won't feel the cold
I'm a fool and, I don't care
I was humiliated; now, it's time to be bold

Your Second Time in Bed

Driving cross-country, takes it out of a man
Around dusk; I lose track of the hours
I get home before supper; when I can
Tonight; I'm riding on thunder showers

You used to run to the door, when I got home
You couldn't wait to take my coat and kiss me
Life was in order, like an old love poem
You were all a woman, had to be

I worked on the Mustang this morning
It showed near forty-one thousand
The light flashed an oil warning
The floor was covered with red, soft sand

Was this morning, your second time in bed?

You don't smile or look at me anymore
I try to hold you, but, you pull away
Where's the laughing eyes, I knew before?
Is it something I said; or didn't say?

The house looks like a tornado, hit it
Beer cans everywhere; dirty TV trays
The dresses you wear; don't even fit
You smell like the bar at Billy Ray 's

The house used to be clean, when I got home
Our kids pretended to do their homework
You've been going out; to cruise and roam
Marriage isn't a responsibility you can shirk

Was this morning, your second time in bed?

Where did the red sand in the car, come from?
The only place it's found, is; Stonewall Park
You love the guy who took you to the prom
You've been seen kissing, in the dark

When I touch you lately; I turn to ice
The bed's not made up like before
Relaxing side by side, was, so nice
I hear; a man visits our back door

Are your tears from sadness, or relief?
I'm the main course, and the dessert, is him
I work hard all week; I don't need this grief
Spill it; chances I'll believe you, are slim

You picked me, over Tommy Hopper?
He was seeing your best friend; Dianne
It looked like a fling; but he didn't drop her
They got married; and moved to Cheyenne

He bought, Wellington's Cotton farm
I heard, he was running for mayor
Lynne; you can do him a lot ofharm
Please let him go, if you really care

I've always been there, for you
You should've told me long ago
I remember our vows; and I've been true
Let's start over; there's no place to go

The blame, isn't yours completely
After all the years, we've been together
I knew the days, weren't closing neatly
Spring's here, I feel a change in weather

I Don't Need Your Kind of Love

I saw you walking down McKenzie Street
Swaying sassy and smiling sweet
No one told me you were home from the city
Your cold good-bye, was a dog-gone pity

You went knocking on my best friend's door
He said I'm the one you still adore
Are you looking for a second chance?
Did your lover, leave you at the dance?

Funny, how you think you know someone
Than; one day, she comes undone
Red pills and needles can change you
You hurt, but there's nothing you can do

I don't need your kind of love!
Gypsy eyes; I don't need your kind of love!

It looks like you're home to stay
You couldn't stand me yesterday
Come down from the sky!
Let it out! Sit down and cry! cry!, cry!

Can you imagine; how I felt?
You kicked my heart, just to see me melt
Remorse is good, if it's real
Why are you here? What's the deal?

Lies are weak and float like air
I'm a liar and I still care
We'll never be the same again
Is all love, this insane?

I don't need your kind of love!
Raven hair; you've bewitched me!

Who knows where this will lead?
I love you, and you 're all I need
To love someone, and be twice betrayed
Is better than being alone and being afraid

I'll take any kind of love All
that matters, is above Mercy
for those who sinned We
have to chase the wind

I need your kind of love

Just Walk Out the Door

Its five o'clock, and the alarm's ringing
Still dark outside, as I struggle to awaken
I swing myself off the bed, my head stinging
My body's aching and my limbs are shaking

Please, Mr. Sunshine; peek over the hills
Bring a song of bluebirds to my mind
I live in a jar surrounded by red, round pills
My life's a joke and love's unkind

It's eight o'clock; another late day
His truck is kicking up gravel
As it swings onto the driveway
Is he riding alone, or with the devil?

God; when will this end?
I open the door with a pasted smile
He'll never love me, why pretend?
My courage is always on trial

The stars in the sky, will watch over me
I know that one day, I'll feel the sun
Is this how it's meant to be?
Missed dinner again, he was having fun

My life's a joke, and *I'm* in a bind
When will the song birds, sing for me?
Why can't I leave this place, behind?
There's a new valley, for me to see

I won't take the hurt today
Guess that I'll just walk out the door
I'll face whatever comes my way
I'm walking, like I never did before

I *won't* take the heartache anymore
He won't find me here, tonight
He gets home at eight; I'll be gone by four
I'm walking out while the sun is bright

Yeah, I'm walking out that door
It's easy; I'll just turn the knob and push
I hear the country music, I adore
light up my Camaro, and; swoosh

Take My Picture off the Wall

I never could, bring home a paycheck
No self-respect, and my life was a wreck
Every morning; my head was on the floor
I couldn't live like that anymore

Aint got much education, to speak of
No one, no more, to give me love
When you're stuck in the mud; get creative
I'll damned well make it; I'm a Texas native

Went and got myself cleaned up
There's a new cafe called, "The Dixie Cup"
The music is fine, but, the beer's finer
I gave a Levi girl; my best one-liner

I aint no fish; but, she's got me hooked
It's something, about the way she looked
I put my rebel past, behind me
She told me, she's from Tennessee

She changed a little; day by day
I don't listen to what people say
Six days at work, made me old and sore
She didn't cook meals, like she did before

Ornery old paint; went and bit my hand
It took two months or more to mend
People at the clinic, sewed me up good
Out of work; I did what I could

She dusted my picture every day
When she opened windows, it would sway
She loved that image on the wall
The frame grew spider webs, that fall

I was getting home earlier those days
Some yahoo, parked his Dodge in my space
The porch door was opened, just a crack
Clothes on the dresser; she was ready to pack

I saw a man's shirt and britches on the bed
He went out the window; I slapped her, instead
"I got a dozen like him; I don't need you at all!"
"I'm gone! Take my picture off the wall!"

"Take my picture off the wall!"
"We're married"
"don't you recall?"

I'm a happier, freer, man today
I learned a brand new way to play
Let your head guide you, not; your heart
Your mind is strong; it can't be torn apart

Take my picture off your wall!
Take my picture off your wall!

Rainy, Please Don't Go

Put your bags down, Rainy!
Step back from that old screen door!
I need you; let's talk it over sanely
Please wait; let's talk some more

The things I said last night
Should never have been said
Stay here 'til the early light
I know we'll both be glad

I hate the way men look at you
The way you move behind the bar
Smiling and serving them their brew
Full house, and; Baby, you're the star

Rainy, please don't go!
Rainy, close the door!

Your eyes are clear and dry
They're looking; straight through me
Go ahead and say good-bye
Maybe, today; was meant to be

I made you cry a hundred times
For things you didn't do
I had no reason, there was no rhyme
Now; I'm losing you

I forced you into waiting arms
That'll hold you differently
His young and manly charms
Will erase all memory of me

Rainy, please don't go!
I love you more than he

Unlock your heart for me
You don't hear the words I say
I don't know how to be free
Stay; tomorrow's a brand new day

I see no tears inside your eyes You
don't care, that our love dies Your life
will be of pink in spring You'll wear
a different diamond ring

Rainy, please don't go! You're
my life and soul mate Sweet
Darling, don't you know? Rainy;
wait! It's not too late!

I heard her trip on the first stair
Those boots are, way, too big for her
Nothing left to say; all I can do, is stare
She was wearing a coat of rabbit fur

Rainy, thank you for the sunny days

She Laughed when I said, "I Love You"

I grew up alone, and I had to be tough
Home, was in the shanty side of town
I had good hands; and I had to be rough
I was small, so, I punched with ever pound

The ring in El Paso, was a money pit
Sneaking in, was easy, anytime
One palooka after another, got his candle lit
I'll try it; I could use an extra dime

By my tenth fight, they knew my name
I slept on a stack of mats at night
My tenacity, was my call to fame
Life was unreal, but boxing was right

My next rumble, was the following week I
lived in the gym, so I saw every fight There
she was; a blond beauty, acting meek She's
too good to ask out, but I just might

I grew up alone, and I grew up tough
Home, was in the shanty part of town
I was good with my hands, I had to be rough
I was small, but, I punched with every pound

Six months later; and I hadn 't met her folks
She asked me to show her where I lived
I steered her away, with a few light jokes
She didn't push it, and I was relieved

All of my friends had met her
She formed a fan club in my name
We didn't go downtown, together
She said, I'd be stolen, with all that fame

She attended El Paso University
I always wanted to visit a college campus
Boredom got the best of my curiosity
I've never had a license; so I took a bus

She sat with a group of people near a pond
They were riding and chasing each other
I called out her name, but she didn't respond
I went to sit, and she said; "don't bother"

I thought she was joking; I didn't understand
Earlier; I said "I love you", to her
She said she wasn 't sure; so, why pretend?
I sat and took it; I've learned to handle hurt

Everyone there, was nervous and surprised
A boy in fancy shorts, pulled her away
The happy times, were just a disguise
I was pissed; I had nothing more to say

I grew up alone and I grew up tough
Home was in the shanty side of town
I was good with my hands, I had to be rough
I was small, but, I punched with every pound

What's going on? I thought she loved me
Everyone has a secret life, including rich girls
She's used to sitting on Daddy's knee
I need sweat and blood; she needs pearls

Let's forgive and forget; I love you She
giggled, than she laughed at me
Chances oftaking you seriously; are few She
pointed and laughed; so all could see

She laughed when I said, "I love you"

That was my first trip out of the hood
I've seen bodies with needles in the arms
I tried to act indifferent, but I never could
I'm real; they're nothing, but plastic charms

I fight for a living, but I know who I am
You can't hide who you are in the ring
A pugilist can't be a wolf dressed like a lamb
When you don't know yourself; you 're nothing

My mother used to tell me:
Son; not everything that glitters, is gold
Test it first, to see
Life, is hurtful, and the truth is cold

Today, I wear the championship belt
I've known players and I've known friendship
Old flames talked about God, but never knelt
My new sloop has sails, that don't fray, or rip

I tripped on my lace, and kissed the canvas
She laughed with me, as she said, "I love you,
Sherry laughed with me, as she said, "I love you,
She kissed my flattened nose, and said, "I love you,

Shadows in the Dark

She was wearing Chane!Number Five
Monterey was chilly and we were alive
The waves caressec; i the rocks below
The night had to go long; it had to go slow

It was dusk, when we reached Carmel Bay
I said less, than I wanted to say
"Unchained Melody", was on the a. m. station
All I felt, was pure elation

The night was cloudy, but the moon was out
We heard the stars talking, right out loud
Vicki was smiling with the wind in her hair
A few more miles, and we'd be there

I didn't want the moment to end
Our love was real, but I couldn't pretend
She reminded me of a girl, long ago
Memories; are like scarecrows in the snow

Navy blue lace, encased the night
The moon was covered, but its glow was bright
I, alone saw it, and I didn 't know why
We were swinging on stars, in the sky

Clouds took the light, and didn 't leave a trace
I drew her close, and my lips -car-essed her face
Tiny arms around my neck, lightly tightened
She clung to me, like she was frightened

Nothing remained, but, shadows in the dark
Shadows in the dark; the night was so, dark

Dreams of tomorrow, washed out to the sea
The ghosts in my soul, will not release me
I'm paying for a love that went, so wrong
I try to forget, but, I'm not that strong

The air was alive, with the scent of Chane!
My mind was clearing, oot; in a spell
The hour was late, and it was colder
Vicki looked young, but, I felt older

We walked hand in hand, that starless night
I wanted to kiss her, but, I had no right
She said something; I hadn't heard in years
Her words, filled my eyes with tears

Shadows in the dark
Shadows of long ago, in the dark

I could hear a song; that I heard before
A message from the past, from one I adore
My new love knew that I kept a secret, and
Not being honest, is my worst regret

I could sense, I was in for a big surprise
The night was yawning; the sun begun to rise
Pacific breezes, reminded me of another place
My heart flew away, to happier days

I remember sun beams and silk in her hair
I wanted to confess my past; but, I didn't dare
My arms embraced her, as she reached for me
She shuddered and sighed, mysteriously

Our kisses were light, in the beginning
She smiled and my head started spinning
There was something, about her name
Are we in paradise, or, in a game?

Shadows in the dark
What are these shadows, in the dark?

My little phantom of the night
Laughed out loud, with sarcastic delight
She started to dance, like in the sixties
Auburn hair in the air; pretty as you please

Vicki, said, "Did I change that much?"
"My sister was your girl in sixty-four"
"I prayed, that one day, we'd touch"
"You left, and I didn't see you anymore"

"Don't you know, that girls, grow up?"
I tried not to speak -or interrupt
"You didn't look at me; you didn't care"
My miracle in May, was too much to bear

"I prayed every day you were in Nam"
"You don't know me or where I'm from"
"I'm not the child, I used to be"
"Dante, you're still you, and I'm still me"

Shadows in the dark
Love doesn't die; it matures

When you laughed; I knew who you were
Everything around me, begin to stir
Vietnam is a memory'; now, I'm with you
You waited for me; your love must be true

If, I'm dreaming; wake me next Christmas
I missed the last boat; this one; won't pass
The shadows in my mind; have a silver lining
The riches in life, require no mining

You've turned shadows into meadows
Life calls us; and, it's time to close
From where, came, those shadows in the dark?

A Morning without Sunshine

I awaken and I thank God for another day
I get ready for work, and I'm on my way
Only bears, and I, get up this early
Fat.'s. f0r the. yQung andtb£. burly

Yesterday's coffee; boils on the stove
Mule deer, grazing in the grove
Oakwood burning; I recall a happier place
The flames in the dark, outline her face

Ran out offlower, running out of flakes
I'll buy more ifl can sell some rakes
Need to batten the barn; winter's coming quick
The Mcintosh and delicious are ripe to pick

Feoce a:rekfsscttre-ground
Drop rocks and gravel all around
I'll trade for a heap of dried beans
With luck, they'll add some greens

Every day, is the same day
How I long to see a sun ray
My sky is cloudy, heavy and dark
Just yesterday, I kissed her in the park

A morning without sunshine

There aren't many reasons to smile
Yesterday; we walked on air, down the isle
That spring, we picked clover in the meadow
Since early June, I've been the only shadow

I'mwasting. ny·life away
I'm a breathing man; not made of clay
It. isn 't sinful tD love again
Where do I go, how do I begin?
                                                    ;
She knew, how I hate to be alone
I've never been a rolling stone
My path to church has turned to ma. olds
I'll build a bridge, where the river folds

My windows are open, to let the world in
Locks of steel, have melted from within
The Lord, works in mysterious ways
He turns Decembers, into Mays

A day without sunshine
Fading clouds of sorrow in my mind
The drapes of mourning are spreading
I walk with the sun, not forgetting

The Brightest Star

I remember April and frosty, starlit nights
She cooked magically, and I tidied up
I still see her smile, amidst celestial sights
She sang, as I sipped Daniels from a cup

She was always the brightest star
The Big Dipper, the North Star and Orion
We can touch them, yet, they're so far
Captured by an archer, Polaris, and a lion

Winking, dancing, swinging wonders
We hold hands, as she dreams and ponders
Streaks of fluorescent light, accent the dark
They didn't touch us; but they left their mark

They have a knighted order of royalty
Like a chorus line; they battle for attention
The brightest, pirouettes first; its only loyalty
The skies don't sparkle; without contention

Even now, I enjoy balmy, fall nights
The shiny dancers have gone to sleep
Someone spun my world and dimmed the lights
I search for her, but Heaven's too deep

Someone told me once; that love, is eternal
Kindred spirits remain together, as mother and child
Vows live through time, like Ann Frank's journal
Mourning is unforgiving, but, memories are mild

Oh, how I love to sit on the porch and star-gaze
I talk to the abyss of the speckled, distant sky
I can see Maria, picking roses in the haze
I go to bed with a tear and star dust in my eye

There's a newer, brighter, star tonight
A new lead dancer, in a celestial chorus line
In the opaque beyond, I see a neon kite
Because ofher, the evening universe, is mine

We're only alone, if we want to be alone
Read by a stream, or walk on the clouds
Peace is found in prayer and, the unknown
Float skyward, separate from the crowds

There's a star, for every one ofus
You'H know, which one belongs to you
It'll be, the brightest star in the chorus
She wears a halo of gold, and blue

Your loved ones, never really leave you
I feel her touch in the morning breeze
She stands beside me, in everything I do
I feel no pain, when I'm on my knees

She's as much alive as last autumn
She just stepped through "the curtain"
My bottle of scotch has no bottom
I'll hold her again; of this, I'm certain

Star bright, star light!

You Can't Handle, My Kind of Love

They all loved you, like your daddy did
Normal relationships, weren't good enough
Vicki; Daddy responded to your every, bid
Will you be able to handle my kind of love?

You were there, the day of the crash
It was my last circuit race at Indy
I lost a lot of blood, and a lot of cash
Gasoline and guts, is all that's in me

I've known good nurses, but, none like you
You did everything, on a military cadence
You sat with me, the whole night through
I can't be one of your needy patients

Our first date, was like a shine on a sneaker
You're used to oysters, lobster and caviar
I like the spice in my food, a little weaker
I need to know, who you really are

You can't handle my kind of love

I'm a patient man, but, don't run me around
You said the others didn't mind
Let's meet in the middle; how does that, sound?
I love you, but I'm not the puppy kind

Love is an art form of give and take
Most doors swing back and forth, evenly
Off-balance relationships; are bound to break
We need to voice opinions candidly

My love for you; is like none before
I'm ready to give you all of me
Can you accept this; or; do I use the door?
Give me the word, and I'll set you free

You can't handle my kind of love
The sun isn't warm, when we're together
Two years wasted; what was I thinking of?
It's cold here; I need a change in weather

You Weren't At the Party

The class of eighty-five graduation
A hotter than Orleans day
No more late bells, no evaluation
I'm as lost, as when I started, anyway

Come one, come all, to Haney's barn!
Hooting and hollering; what a dust cloud!
Flags and balloons, strung up with yam
Guitars were screaming, long and loud

You broke up, over a silly idea
Your sister kissed me, all on her own
I was busy with the beer and sangria
I smiled, and told her to leave me alone

Things aren't always, how they appear
You used to trust me, what happened?
Your mind was someplace else; it's clear
Was there a college bash, to attend?

Had you outgrown me, Kate?
You didn't dress, like you did before
You left early and got home late
I didn't see you by your door

You were in a red Jaguar that night
Your shades were too big for you
The scarf!gave you, flew like a kite
Nothing was said; but, I knew

You ran away with an Auburn senior
You didn't stop to say, good-bye
We heard from you twice last year
Is there a knot, you plan to tie?

Someone in your family; drew me in
Little sisters tend to grow up too
We're a lot closer than we've ever been
She's smart, and deeper than I knew

The engagement party, was in June
Everyone was there; but you
The wedding was under Montana's moon
The flowers were turquoise; your color's blue

You weren't at the party, Kate
You missed this one too

The Way She Looks At Me

I'm no Johnny Cash, but
I'll pass in a crowd, most days
My ride, is a fifty-seven Nash
I'm young, but set in my ways

I haven't had success with women
I won't settle; unless she's right for me
She doesn't 't exist; I'm only dreaming
I'll wait; if that's how it has to be

The way she looks at me
Seven-Eleven, is my first stop of the day
"Howdy Slim Pickens, what'll it be?"
I love it when she looks at me that way

Coffee warms my innards, delightfully
I'm a jittery hopper, when I'm close to her
She flirts with blue eyes; most skillfully
My attempts at dialogue; are just a slur

Women have said, they love me
Pretty words, but, eyes tell the true story
Rhetoric; empty words without honesty
It's time to start living, and not worry

I saw her on the customer side of the counter
Jean dress, sandals and a yellow bandana
Among the Saturday crowd; I found her
She was with friends, Vicki, Jill and Brenda

On the way to Clear Lake; I pulled over
"Amy, why do you look at me, that way?"
"I once gave you a bouquet of Irish clover"
"You kissed my cheek, that early May"

"I've loved you as long, as I can remember"
"To you; I was the little girl next door"
"This child; turned nineteen, in September"
"I'm right here; what are you waiting for?"

I love the way, she looks at me

I'm Done Begging

I didn't mean to call you by her name
I loved her, long before I met you
You call me Rick; the blame's the same
I apologized to you, what else can I do?

I'm done begging, Stacey!
We forgive strangers for indiscretions
I'm done begging
Do we leave in different directions?

I picked Tracy for the Dallas trip
That was in our junior year; let it go
I try to explain, but all I get is lip
I'm true, if you really want to know

I'm done begging!

I'm the first, to accept you as you are The
hopper you were dating, was a child He
broke your heart, just to tug on the scar
You yelled at Tracy, just because she smiled

I didn't mean to call you by her name
She's the only one I've loved since you
You called me Rick, so, the blame's the same
I apologized; I'm sorry, what else can I do?

We all live in the same world except you
Your planet's bigger, so you look down on us
Fathers leave families every day, it's nothing new
You went to school in a Porsche, now it's a bus

Step out of you bubble and look around
We have problems, but, we don't blame everyone
Your feet are flying, but you belong on the ground
Talk to us; our love doesn't have to be won

I'm done begging, Stacey; I'm done begging

I know why you plead for attention
Your mother doesn't know you're there
She didn't question your detention
Let's all disappear into thin air

We were ready to walk away from you
You're too young to be afraid
Trust in us, we'll pull you through
Doors will open, and roads can be made

That smile, belongs on "Seventeen", magazine
This is the real you; laughing and carefree
No apologies; we don't play that scene
I'm with you; there's a tomorrow; kiss me

Kiss me again; do I have to beg?

Stone Honey

We were both nine or ten
She was a little bundle of honey
Life by the river, was exiting then
Time changed her; how sad, how funny

Life shapes *us*, like a sculptor and his vision
Results reflect, the mastery of the artist
The North Star's missing; *for,* no reason
I tripped on life; but, she fell hardest

Stone honey

Honey doesn't spoil easily
Midnight; I don't care if I wake the town It's
been ten years, but; she'll know, it's me She
was cute, in her; "Minnie Mouse", gown

She expected me to appear
She spoke my name, in a whimper, half crying
We reached for each other, no caution, *no,* fear
Her face was pale; her eyes; were dying

We sat by the fireplace, 'til the sun lit the room She
went off to college, half *grown,* half educated Her
roommate, liked parties; her *room,* was a tomb She
gradually, became popular and emancipated

Stone honey

You don't mount a bronco, if you've never ridden
Her freedom, became a run at Daytona
Her love was free; nothing was hidden
Kiss a man twice, and he wants to own 'ya

Sweet and innocent, a frightened freshman
Taste of youthful dill, upon her lips
Torn and shredded sails, mending on dry land
I cleaned her tears, with trembling finger tips

Quiet girls, don't do well in school
A recipe, where nature's honey, turns to stone
Innocence; the first ingredient in making a fool
Life experiences, aren't always home-grown

Trust is gone; she stares, like a she- wolf
When you're naked in the cold, you harden
She was tiny; a butterfly on a tulip, so aloof
You'll find prickly things in every garden

We skipped stones across the lake, yesterday
The morning sun, daffodils, and hair of amber
She laughed, when my stone sank right away
Her kisses taste like honey, as I remember

Sweet, golden, warm, honey; in a little cup

I Once Met a Lady

The sun was shining brightly in the antique store
There, you can discover, a brand new yesterday
I saw her; she was all I wanted, and more
She looked at me and, I didn't know what to say

You can't feel normal; ifyou 're stung by ninety bees
My face is like a Disney comic; anyone can read it
I was glowing like neon, from my nose to my knees
She realized my situation, and, I felt like an idiot

Anyone could see, she was amused by my reaction
The lady in the long, blue dress, just stood and smiled
I extended my hand and swallowed my indignation
Her brief introduction, was lady-like and mild

I don't recall having such a good time, just talking
As we talked about similarities; her eyes widened
She was smooth and controlled, like a jaguar stalking
When she talked about rock; her voice heightened

I once met a lady

I asked if she was hungry, and she said, <'I'm starved"
 She paid for her album and I; for a picture ofDietrich
We went where salami and provolone, are freshly carved
We sat at a cozy booth, with a jukebox in reach

I didn't have enough quarters for the music
She emptied her purse on the table
The chewed Juicy Fruit, was making me sick
This is my best date; not a Nora Roberts fable

We were raised differently, but, the same
I'm a New Mexican roper; she's Ohio's upper crust
She said, we'd marry, but intends to keep her name
Names don 't really matter; someday, we'll all be dust

My mother had a, «Norge" washer with a roller
Didn't matter how much ((Blue Cheer", soap was in it
Light colors stayed light and dark colors, got bolder
This world won't change; no matter how you spin it

Powder sugar and red chili, don't agree
You can experiment and fuss, all you want
One can't always be whom he wants to be
When you know you can't score; punt

I hang out at the same antique store
Last time I was there, blue eyes spoke to me
Who knows; I might meet someone else to adore
Understand their signals; check your glossary

I don't know about you, but; I once met a lady there

An Odd Sock

Everyone has at least one odd sock
Have you ever used a sock to dust a clock?
All the other stockings match two-by-two
Every drawer has a few, some old, some new

Why do we keep these argyle orphans?
A loner sock doesn't have many fans
We try to match them with other socks
Sooner or later; they're dumped in a box

Even odd things have a purpose
They hold memories and are useful to us
When they were new, you wore them proudly
You proclaimed their comfort, loudly

As years go by, old things mean a lot to us
I still have my G.I. Joe and Tonka bus
Years ago, my toys were the style of the day
School was fun, but I couldn't wait to play

Age creeps up on us too quickly
We lose interest in things we do weekly
I think of happier times, and in a while
I see children playing; and I smile

Is a sock that doesn't match, really odd?
Brothers are different, but have the same blood
Why must we look the same to be accepted?
Heroes weren't always, what we expected

Einstein, Lincoln and Patton; to name a few
Without them; we would have to start anew
They walked a path that was less traveled
Why do we judge? I'm all unraveled

What does an odd sock, have to offer? Ask any golfer!
Without wooly bags with moth holes and snags
We'd label every club with ribbons and tags

Let's all, be a little odd! It's okay, really!

Twice Loved

Summer days longer than those in Alaska
Can't catch footballs on a quicksand beach
Tripping; watching a girl from Nebraska
Long hair bright, white, no need for bleach

Windy waves, champagne uncorked Salt lye
in the eye; turn your back, Fella Violet rays
bake you like honey ham, forked Running,
clash with breeze, fall on umbrella

Nebraska girl smiling at me; a fence of pearls
Bikinis, tiny jelly bean colored hammocks
Filled with; hour-glass, giggling girls
Polka dot tops, on radiating beach rocks

August, like hare chased by beagle; outran July
Pretties from far-away places, touch the bases
Kissing boys on the sly; under a starless sky
Fly away, with not much to say; to home oasis

Surfer massages slick board, with heels of feet
Mind near the moon, with his loony loon
Contest at Maverick, but he can't compete
The groovy little pills wore out too soon

Wants the cup; can't net it, best forget it
It won't fit on top of thirty others, anyway
Summer's over; stop the flying; or regret it
Iowa girl, moved in next door yesterday

Junior high cupcake, first kiss at Pinto Lake
Shaking boy unsteady on Sears flat bottom boat
Cutie Trudy; isn't shy; make no mistake
Best to kiss her as she reaches for her coat

Twice loved

Redheaded, Santa Cruz boy on Cape Cod shore
Little New Englander, skipping by, sneaking a peek
City girl, mature beyond her years; not out to explore
Girl on my street, eyes like stilettos, she's not meek

I'm not a good juggler; good-bye to one; but, which?

One is Belgian chocolate, dark and tart; like Cher
Love at a distance loses direction in the air waves
The east; it takes a life's savings to go there
I'll stay close to home; "he is wise; who saves"

Thirsty; I need a drink of freedom on the rocks
Girl, next door; knee-high bobby socks, lilac shades
Plymouth Rock, honey visits, but seldom knocks
California girls, wear Lakota-Shawnee braids

It would've been wasted time, for freedom writers
If I would surrender my liberty to a girl
I don't want marriage, taxes and ankle-biters
My days are for bird-dogging and shooting the curl

Twice loved

Too Many Women

I see a woman tall and slight and sure
She wears a crown of Moroccan gold
I'm enchanted by her Lilith-like, allure
I would summon her near, ifI were bold

Like a silver fox; she dwells in the meadow
Merry zephyrs, dance in the fields ofwheat
She waltzes alone; just she, and her shadow
She sings, but I know not, the mystic beat

She's a sunray, after a storm in early May
She dances with Alessandra Ferri; in Milan
Models the rarest diamonds from Bombay
Have you seen her mansions in Ceylon?

Phoenician lady, sent to tempt me
She's gone with the sunset; much like youth
I had a dream; that came to me gently
It was exaggerated and much too smooth

I'm an old-fashioned, Gatsby era romantic
My heart's in a village, somewhere in Holland
I haven't found her on the Pacific, or the Atlantic
She's not on the seas, so; I'll scout the Highlands

Women; are monoliths of humility and character
How can we not adore, God's perfect creation?
They know us; Don Juan, true-blue, or actor
Tell me why a woman, can't lead this nation

This is an ode to all women, past and present Imagine
civilization, without sensibility and satin Victors had a
woman at their side; which haven't? They penned,
"Social Order" and, they hold the patent

Women outnumber men, on this spinning toy
Have you ever wondered, why?
They clean the mess, when there's nothing left to destroy
Listen to them, praise them, learn; the limit is the sky

We have too many women; keep them coming!

Shoot Twice

Strike one, strike two, you're out!

Life is just a game of chance
I'11 tell you what it's all about
You don't score, with just one glance
If she can't hear you talking; shout

Love at first sight, isn't always real
Your life can't change, on the first look
You think that blonds; are all ideal
Get your head together; read the book

Read, the "Book of Love"
Learn your lessons from above
Love doesn't come easy
You need to try, until you're dizzy

It 's too early to throw the rice
Wait, for the right time of year
She'll tease you, and she'll entice
Be patient; the time is near

If you don't win her with the first shot
Than; shoot twice
Shoot twice, Charlie Brown! Shoot twice!

Love is just a game that's played
It too, has rules and limits
Her kisses are strategically delayed
Ifyour heart-light's too bright; dim it

She may not be playing in your field
Show her the one; that better suits her
Say something Latin, to make her yield
Give her the ring, if she needs a booster

We rarely get them with the first shot
Make sure that she's the one for you
You'll wish and hope and pray a lot
Make sure, your aim is true

If you miss the first time
Shoottvnce, shoottvnce
If you want her bad enough
Shoot twice

If she feels the same; you'll know
She'll come in April, or in May
She'll be yours, in sunshine or in snow
Don't blow this thing, don't delay

Always, shoot twice!
Ifyou don't score; someone else, will
Shoot twice!

Too Shy To Dance

I was born in Providence, twenty years ago
Cool, is for a fool; I don't do anything slow
Like a badger; I have a Dixie state of mind
I'm not a Puritan; obedient and half blind

The South smells like freedom and cold beer
Nightlife: steel guitars and fiddles in the air
A sign read: "Make new friends, this year"
I want to dance; but, I think they'll stare

Too shy to dance; brother; too shy to dance

My table was small and wobbly, near the floor I
moved like dirty laundry, in a ringer washer
Man! I've never heard music like this, before
! Pretty girl in faded Lees; I just had to watch her

I wanted company, so; I started to look around
Realized that looking; wasn't like touching
Southern girls, fly close to the ground
I'll find one that's alone; no sense in rushing

I said, "Hello, I'm Dan and I'm new here"
She pushed her hat up, and looked at me
'Tm Ashleigh; I'm not as native, as I appear"
"Drove down here, from south ofBeverly"

The two-step; looks great, is it hard to learn?
I don't know, but this is a great time to try
When do we slide and when do we tum?
I'm no Fred Astaire; I can't step very high

We were tenderfoots at a hoe-down
Both of us, were too shy to dance
Blue grass deliciousness, in a country town
Dusty jeans, dancing with pricy, fancy pants

Papa told me, I wouldn't learn by looking
All those flying feet; learned by doing
Glide just a little bit; now, you're cooking
Nobody 's laughing, and nobody's booing

Not too shy to dance

That was a rainy night, long ago; look at us now
We don't go dancing alone anymore
When it 's over; she curtsies and I bow, somehow
We know every inch of that red oak floor

Aint too shy to dance!

I'm Ready

When I was thirteen; Rosie liked me
My mind was in playing and cutting school
A year later; she asked me what I wanted to be
I told her that I want to be a pro at pool

I'm ready

At fifteen, she asked me to hold her hand I
told her I was jamming late, that night She
sang in a choir; I played lead in a band
I was choking; she was holding on too tight

When I was sixteen, she didn't visit anymore
I made new friends in quick succession
A few months later; my bed became a floor
That July; I was drunk at my own court session

Life was there for *me,* and I was ready
I did what boys that age; do
I played my guitar; no time for going steady
No self-respect; I lost it in some bayou

I'm ready

When I was seventeen, we were at the top
Twenty-four hours on the clock; we worked forty
I was shooting sixteen grams, *and,* Icouldn't stop
I tried to play football, but, I didn't feel sporty

When I turned eighteen, I forgot the notes
I *was,* "Pop-Eye", walking on conveyor belts
The stages were wobbling, inner tube boats
I went to Norway, to see how ice melts

My brothers showed me a high school movie
Playing air guitar and prancing like Jagger
We were dressed like hippies and acting groovy
I was dancing straight; not once; did I stagger

My mother cried; to see what I've become
She saw Rosie with a new friend, last Friday
Rosie hugged her and called her, "Mom"
 She asked, when I'll come home to stay

I'm ready

Life is going by too fast, and I'm scared
I'm not smart enough to go it alone
Look at my life now; see how I faired
I'll talk to her, but, I won't use a phone

No more booze, no more weed, no dust
The mirror, doesn't reflect who I really am
No more devil whispers, not even a gust
She's engaged, but; I don't give a damn

One drop of Indian ink; paints the world, ebony
 It falls on one small spot, than it quickly spreads
Why didn't I choose to live; in harmony
It's my fault my loved *ones*, hang their heads

I'm ready

I've been living in the bad part of town
I can't move forward, behind a locked door
What will it feel like, to touch the ground?
I want her to love me, like she did before

I'm ready

Try Me, You'll like Me

Oh, what a party! What a screaming party! We
were sliding and jumping, like Jackson
That Saturday night; I drank and danced hardy
Some were late, but didn't miss the action

No one at the Ritz; no hopping at the Carlton
No one cares; if you're uncool, or act the clown
They're swinging mighty in South Hamilton
Tonight; I'm dancing slow; in Memphis town

Try me, you'll like me

You looked fine; in your fish net stockings
A foot too short; faded, Lee shorts
The crimson blouse; was pleasantly shocking!
You danced all night, and tried other sports

It was cool, but; you were going home with me
You turned, and saw, how I was looking at you
They all reached for you: one, two and three
"Sorry boys! There's something, she has to do"

You said, I was fine, and I could dance
How could you see me in the smoky, light?
I saw you in the crowd with, just one glance
I needed a dancing partner, that April night

Try me, you 'll like me

You're bright; but, you're full of illusions You
think I'm rich, and have looks to spare
Observant; but you've jumped to conclusions
Before you go hunting, Girl; learn how to snare

I'm ten persons, I'm six and I am one
You want to soak me, like a rainy season
Only with patience, can a man be won
You want me; but, I haven 't seen the reason

Try me, you'll like me

I'm not the rocker, you think you know
Saturday; I was in a celebration situation
The real me; is in this diary, tied with a bow
I date girls, but; they're just an imitation

Now, I'm standing here, beside you
I've turned myself in, and turned myself out
This man will be; a shiny hue ofblue
Turn and walk; if you have a doubt

Tell me if you're unhappy with who I am
I've been waiting for you, since junior high
What good is Texas toast, without the jam?
We can sing on rooftops, and dance in the sky

You've read my personal book
Do you see a shy kid with "high-water" pants?
The new me; is: witty, degreed, and I can cook
I don't mess with liquor or illegal plants

Try me, you'll like me

I stood in line, at all the dances
You always, picked someone else
This isn't about a crush and teen romances
I hope I reached you; my logic usually sells

Girls that age; are busy finding themselves
They're looking through the eyes of children
Minds were between womanhood, and elves
You kissed some boys, but, they all ran

In youth; love spins us like plastic worlds
I'm still turning like a rooster weather vane
If you don't ask for diamonds, or pearls
We'll have a house, on Primrose Lane

"Try me, Brenda Lee; you'lllike me"
"Try me, Gene Pitney; you'lllike me"

A Cactus, Can Flower Too

Dad told me, that not having a dream
Is like time ending forever; the next day
Reality isn't temporary, it's not a scheme
Son, decide where you fit best; and stay

I wasn't picked for the marching band
Tom Hawkins made it; he's no jewel
I'm short; but, I can give the band a hand
Ah, cobalt uniforms; they look so cool

I've tried track, wrestling and baseball
I'm as fast, as the fastest miler
I pinned my opponents on the first fall
The baseball team, calls me; "cleat-filer"

A cactus, can, blossom too
Everything, in its own time

Ma, what can I do, to be accepted?
Give the people, what, they want!
"Danny DeVito"; isn't neglected
When you can't score, Son; punt!

Not everyone's cut out for sports
Athletes, only play to win popularity
Most can't walk; check the reports
They're male; there ends the similarity

You played guitar when you were eight
Do something with it; make a difference
Get on it; you love it; it's not too late
Don't just leave it hanging on a fence

A cactus, can bloom, too
A cactus can make you stop and look

We played at the Galaxy Rink, last night
Man, we sprayed the crowd with sound
It wasn't cordial; and it wasn't light
We're the meanest band around

The group is, "The Electric Storm"
The band members; are all sizes
We were in outrageously, rare form
It shakes you up; and it mesmerizes

Recognition makes things flow a lot easier
Just put the right foot in the right shoe
We're brand new, but we're getting busier
Even popular kids, want to be on the crew

We have a date at a Nashville studio
A cactus can flower too
They want to launch us, on the radio
A cactus can flower too

Ode to the South

Utopia born of righteous principles
World leader, representative of liberty
Constitution; wisdom of ancient oracles
Come, ye persecuted and be free

Infant nation set and waiting to receive
All voyagers with heartbeats; welcome!
Feel the warmth of a different sun
Speak your mind; your chance will come

Did pilgrims accept the constitution?
The voyagers had never seen a formal school
Learn all you can in a democratic nation
A representative government, is the rule

Elect representatives; voices of the masses
House of Commons; justice and equal votes
A new society divided by three classes
Elite citizens and the banks hold the notes

Mind-tailoring, forms a new way of living
Economy industrial, economy agricultural
Ivory Coast pawns; spiritually torn; forgiving
Was Northern slavery, more natural?

Presidential letters; proclaiming equal rights
Self-government, free speech, be American
Decree to abolish slavery; the fury it invites
Start a brand new country, if you can

There is no family in a home of dissension
Different minds, few ideas, no mutual ground
Civil war declared; our future's in contention
Cannons at Ft. Sumner; that whistling sound

Ghosts in Manassas and Atlanta; why!
The wind screams yet, in Boston and Concord
Sons of southern states, rebelled only to die
Blue and grey; destiny in hands of the Lord

No hatred in gladiators fighting a pointless war
Kill or be killed; too late for compromise
World spinning too fast; put it where it was before
Siblings, same mother; brotherhood in their eyes

In this land; pursue happiness your own way
Human rights; proclaimed, by the highest court
Southern minds; thoughts of secession, at bay
Forsake a culture! To what does Dixie, resort?

What man can tell another how to live?
Mechanize; be better off than you are
Dixie gave all; there's nothing left to give
African soldiers remained under chain and bar

One nation! Whimsical utterances of dreamers
Live by standards of the wealthy states
Bring on the carpetbaggers and schemers
Who rebuilds the smoldering, ashen estates?

Two in battle, is twice the fault
One arrow pointing south; one, the opposite
Blue will pillage. Gray; no bacon, com or salt
Confederates branded rebels, dispose of it!

War's not a tug-a-war to see who's stronger
Phoenix ascended, feathers smoldering and bent
Who was American, who was the monger?
We fought and died; the verdict's been sent

The question, therefore; remains:
What, in Heaven; have we learned?
The truth; will forever dwell in the rain
Who was the U.S.A? Why was Atlanta burned?

Time passes, and all with it fades from memory
An era of courage and terror remain in our soul
Our past lies in a soup bowl we call history
We stand in the shadow of what yesterday stole

Cotton fields, weevils, apple pie and watermelon
Textiles, steamships, tractors and new ideas
Let's gather 'round and sip humility by the gallon
Unity is the answer; but, only love can free us

Cotton Doesn't Grow Here, Anymore

I still recall sensations of walking on clouds
We used to play in Hurley's cotton fields
I wanted to live forever; but, I had my doubts
Home was changing through secret land deals

That was a long, long time ago
Cotton doesn't grow here anymore
This isn't the South we used to know
Our thorny friend grows on a different shore

Prospecting is changing the face of our nation
Day in and day out they strip the mountain side
Willy's Produce was here; now, it's a toll station
I see rolling highways, but it's not the same ride

Where can I find virgin, American land?
Cotton doesn't grow here anymore
Industrialist have bought the upper hand
No lakes or ponds to fish in, like before

My God! Where have our plantations gone?
Earth foundations, where once; palaces stood
The nightingale now sings a lonely song
I'd bring it all back ifI could; If only I could

Carpetbaggers unsheathe their steely knives
Reconstruction was meant to bring rebirth
The constitution is our protectorate of lives
It's our guaranty for rights on Earth

Cotton doesn't grow here, anymore
Did you hear; do you know?
They built a brand new grocery store
It was my lower forty; a year ago

Someone put a canvas cover on the sun
Sycamore and eucalyptus look bent and old
I'm a son ofDixie, and I wasn't raised to run
We can stand again; ifwe're vigilant and bold

I see a bright horizon of green and white
I see people and cotton in the light
Black and white, picking with all their might
I dreamed of cotton fields last night

God! I dreamed the South will live again
I stooped and picked and, I was color-blind
Before we see puffs of white, we have to begin
There's a better view of tomorrow, from behind

Cotton blossomed again in my dreams
Our Mississippi loam, hasn't changed
Let's drop some seed; it's later than it seems
We'll wake up, to find Heaven rearranged

I saw a hundred cotton fields in the news
Barges filled with pure Egyptian cotton
We've plowed our fields, we've paid our dues
Our peaches are blessed; all else; is rotten

I saw Dixie in a, "pony trap" carriage
She was enrobed in black and white
It's time for understanding, not disparage
A new day is at our door; I see the light

I love you, Dixie

Two Men in Red and Blue

The anchor lamp gave just enough light to see
    the print on the "English Bible"
The war was violent and unpredictable
In the midst of cannon and gun smoke;
    we didn't know friend from rival

This brotherhood consists of immigrants from all
    nations of the world and the native people, but;
    it was never explained to me; why we chained,
    the visitors from Africa

We're Baptist, fourth generation North Carolinians
In school; we learned about our country
I understood the revolutionary war
I understood the French and Indian war

Self- defense becomes necessary, when a sovereign
    government is encroached upon, either by political
    methods; or armed aggression by a foreign entity
Those born here are Americans to the core
The world's political instability requires that
    we maintain armaments in every city

The Union and the Confederacy, Fort Sumner
A rude awakening for a dormant America

One day you're trading pork for lamb with your
    neighbor; that June, you greet your last summer
Mutual, but unclear incivility over slaves and labor
Those days crackled, like a hundred fourth-of-Julys

There's no still in the night, as we hear agonizing
   screams for medics
Infantry on their knees like dogs, searching with their
   hands because Calamity; flew by and took away
   their eyes
The North is armed with the latest from Springfield,
   the South carried shoulder relics

The sounds once thirty fields away, are now at our
   front door
Like locust and other plagues; they *can't* be ignored
In the midst of bugled instructions; we hear a *cry*, no;
   a whimper!

In the yard close to the swine and hens, is a crouching
   form, carrying a man upon its back; my Lord!
A piece of a man's forehead is missing
I see a cut, but Idon't know where it ends
I reached blindly for spirits blended into the night
Ten steps forward, two men wailing at my feet
We had wounded bodies down and unable to fight
I pulled them inside to breathe another day, or; our
   maker to meet

Red like the curse on the Nile at of Exodus Crimson,
   like the robe of Caesar; was the floor The moment
   for decisive action; stares at us Drops of muddy
   tears, mucus and gore

Dawn; like slow motion arrows of noon, recharges
    our minds
"Unhook the shutters, so we may see this mess
of humanity"
"Father; their uniforms are blue, they're not ours!"
    "I only care for these boys; clothing, is just their
    leaders' vanity"

"The more I gaze upon them, the more they look like
    all other boys"
''They breathe the same; they love life as we do"
''They bathe and frolic in early spring showers"
"I hate them no more than I hate you"

Businessmen and politicians behind bronzed doors,
    brewed this apocalypse
How strange it is; that I see none such; carrying a
    musket and a backpack
They profess civil rights, but, deceit and venom,
    coat their lips
Southern leadership was superb; it was Northern
    wealth, they lacked

Southern youth who plow the Earth having no taste
    for bondage; ride on backs of rail-road cars; clack,
    click, clack
Color is not the measure of a man, when all souls are
void of light
Congolese and Kenyan bear no hatred; they just want
    their freedom back
If this nightmare, was about slavery; what took so
    long, for the blacks to fight?

Who is triumphant; when wheat fields on both sides
    turn to graveyards?
Two, perhaps three centuries, will pass, before the
    memory of this war, would have vanished
There will come a day, when we need not, weapons
    of destruction for safe guards
I pray for a day, when war, is like a fallen civilization
    swilled by the sea

All children are born equal, and with their own identity
Some dress in blue and gold, some dress in gray, so bold
See the children, across, the river?
List the many things that make them different
No differences? Not one? Good, perhaps we're learning

Brotherhood isn't another name for, "rainbow"
The spectrum has nothing to do with our souls
Turtles have various shapes and colors
When's the last time you saw a turtle war?

Our shells vary in pigmentation, and just look at the
    mess we've created
Within all of us; the lines are perfect parallels
In this place of freedom; why is that so hard to see?
Angels in Heaven, see with perfection
We have the same eyes, but we choose not to see

I pray for the day, when our flag of fifty-two; equals one
I pray for the day, when, "Ole Glory", has stripes of
    brown
Let's pray for a banner with the gray of an autumn cloud
Let's pray for a banner with the purity of white
Red; is for the blood of all our heroes, in every war

My brother; have we not seen enough red?

The Bridge at Shiloh

Breckenridge County, Murfreesboro, Tennessee
In the Lord's year; eighteen hundred and sixty-two
Preeminence of more lethal engagements, yet to be
Two sides celebrate victory; but, who vanquished who?

This evil serpent ofbloodletting; awakened a year ago
A confederation of gray; targets a horizon, that's blue Why
war? Only the "top-hats" and sissy britches, know
My body's numb; I'll wake it quick, with mountain dew

I remember, when our Stones River journeyed in peace
In late autumn, we heard her splashing against the rocks
Country folk, would visit across the ripples with ease
Boats were rigged like fish on a string; on mossy docks

Barges, floating in all directions on the Cherokee River
Our mills were known everywhere, for quality and price
Anything but Gibraltar, the pan-bottoms could deliver
God's peach pie! Grand Daddy owns a big, fat slice

This territory, looked too industrial, to be Southern
We made beavers look like, they were in hibernation
War was raging; we had no time to be bothering
Talk in the air 'bout separation and emancipation

We were just children, being children, in those days
The Shiloh Bridge had ropes tied, to its bottom side
That was long ago, and today; my mind 's in a haze
Swinging and letting go, was pure, foolish suicide

Up at five; oatmeal, and on the cotton before six
Every picker lugged the same size, gunny bag
Bees and mosquitos; we were free lunch for ticks
What I couldn't carry, late day; I had to drag

Ah, but there was a light at the end of the rows
Nothing like a good ole skinny dip in the Stones River!
There was cool spring water, where the willow grows
Untie the ropes! We done caught the swinging fever!

The river was jam-packed with kids of all ages
At times; I couldn't decide whether to watch or jump in
The Shiloh Bridge was aging; I could see the changes
Today; happy memories, make me start a' smiling

A friend is one who gives and keeps on giving
Our bridge, was the connection to kin on the other side
The Shiloh is a gift from God; that's what I believe in
Folks from all over; came here on their Sunday ride

Blue was out to vanquish everything gray
Infernos licking the sky; were once wheat fields
Locust from hell; couldn't have hurt us that way
Root cellars provided the rest of our meals

We stood helpless as they torched our mills Gone; is
our history, and the future of our sons After their
fill of lightning; they destroyed the stills
The church was ablaze; but, no one drew their guns

The horizon was the painting; "Dante's Inferno"
We stood hand-in-hand at both ends of our bridge
Our faces glistened in the flickering red and yellow
We had no militia, but, we had unity and courage

A young Union officer, tall in the saddle
His face was outlined by the dancing flames
Dusty, but together; this man had seen battle
I recall when war, was just in children's games

They disappeared in a red, mushroom of dust
We bowed our heads and knelt, cried and prayed
Even in war, soldiers can be forgiving and just
I still feel the courage and the pride, we displayed

Yesterday, our town stood proud and strong
Now; it's reminiscent of a spent giant on one knee
We're at their mercy now; but, not for long
We'll rebuild our honor; Texas to the Red Sea

Skeletons of charcoal and tin roofs; stand and stare
Trees, like burned match sticks, heads hanging down
Procrastination, self -pity, hatred; don't dare!
I see Dixie, wearing a long, white gown

We see scars of battle, and remnants of our identity
Our Shiloh stands proudly; swaying in the sun
A living monument representing pride and infinity
Evil has vanished from this land; a new day has begun

We'll erect monuments, for all heroes perished
Our medal is our bridge; and it stands proudly to this day
The memories of resiliency will always be cherished
As Moses in Egypt; our Shiloh saved us that early May

There's a bridge named "Shiloh", over the Stones River
Not to be confused with the any other bridge
We have a bridge named, "Shiloh"
It watches over us. It gives its back to us

I saw Dixie this morning
She was wearing a long, white, cotton gown
How, she shined!
I saw Dixie, this, fine morning

Blue, Gray and Yellow

Unit flags and horse flesh burning
   I smell it, I wear it
Dark skies consume us like a
   Midwestern dust storm
Souls gone to Heaven today
They're better off; I swear it
Screams for mercy, unheard
Soldiers return to dust forms

Two armies in tomato soup Spiced
with gray and blue cotton Blue
uniforms, compasses pointing
   dead south
Gray uniforms; a history not forgotten
Three years ofbrother against brother
   will there be a forth?

Cannons spewing hell of all description
An efficient form of genocide Fires of
terror ignite the night Showers of
meteors crashing to Earth
Field of death; trembling with explosions
Head-high lines of shrapnel; no place to hide
Varying ideas, no ideas; most accept
   we're brothers from birth

"Dear God; why must I kill my brother;
    I don't thirst for war!"
"Yesterday, I plowed and seeded my fields"
"Today, I have to kill; please tell me why"
"God, if I don't vanquish my brother today;
    I will be terminated; what's in store?"
"To say that my heart holds hatred for them;
    would be, a blasphemous; lie"

Young Memphis soldier, conscientious objector
Crucified amidst drum rolls, tears and prayers
Kaleidoscope at dawn; crimson, golden clouds
Northern blue, Southern gray, stars, and stripes
Indigo industrial America; casualties in the field
    like war supplies, stacked in layers
Gray with tired eyes, no victorious march home
No horses prancing, no swords drawn, no pipes

Every general, every mule tender, every medic
    gray or blue, knew the futility of this war
Purely political reasons for the apocalyptic order
Honor bound; the cream of America, submitted
Young and aged, in line for uniforms and weapons
Terrified to the core
Those with polio, bones deformed, loss of limb
All will fight, none exempted

True blue; twice as many on the ground
The gray will take the day
Yellow won't shift either or any way
Aiming at ground; brother won't kill brother
Trembling in the sanctuary of their fox holes

Charge in force! Keep moving forward!
Many will go astray, this day
Yellow will die, for a cause they don't behold
Death will visit, where they were born
The blue, the gray; and the yellow
All brothers, kinfolk, genocide under order

The meek, shall inherit the Earth
Turn the other cheek; don't take either side
Straddle the border lines
The truth is; all war gods are atheists at birth
Recruits fled in terror, in their own defense

They broke under attack and like rabbits;
    ran for the safety of burrows
Why do some run when most stand fast?
Man is born with the instinct to fight or fly
Those who stood; died in rows, rows, rows
The valiant fell, defending Christian beliefs
They weren't the first, or the last

Those who fled died from "friendly" fire
Yellow?
Everyone in war is terrified, are we all cowards?
Is seeking shelter from a hurricane unpatriotic?
The Blue, the Gray and the Yellow
The victims were those who couldn't pay their
    way out
Our brothers in uniform, our country; America

This New Mexico Cowboy; Loves Dixie

Who do you want to be, today? I'll
be Wyatt; you can be the Kid Let's
be in Kansas City, far away We'll
ride like, "cow punchers", did

Hey, Ray! Your turn to choose!
I like Nick Adams, the "Rebel"
He aint no cowboy; you lose!
You're a blue rock; I'm a gray pebble

This New Mexico cowboy; loves Dixie
I know where to find down-to-earth folks
Give me Spanish moss and a magnolia tree
Share, tea, mint juleps and witty jokes

Mark Twain books, made me a dreamer
I love the Mississippi and its paddle boats
The way west, was navigated by steamer
Blame the South for cozy cotton coats

This cowpoke's heart is in Dixie

Hatred doesn't really exist in mankind
I believe that ignorance takes the pulpit
"Bible" education, will cleanse your mind
Don't judge another's life; you didn't live it

People in the southwest, welcome everyone
Be ready to dive into tamales and Spanish rice
Southerners are inviting; like an Orleans dawn
Join a lobster bake; a smile's, the price

A visit to Savannah, was my walk in paradise
Southern mansions glow, like the Parthenon
Spiced lemonade and melon; cold as ice
I'll touch Georgia sun, before my time is gone

I write about the southern celebration of life
Teachers rarely lecture about the bayou region
I had to go to Dixie, to find my wife
We live where pride and integrity; is religion

Time and destiny, takes us from desert to shore
I rode a mare in the sky, with the Gray Ghost
The south has given all; and still, it gives us more
This is the culture of grace and the perfect host

From New Mexico to Birmingham, with love
You have a cotton-loving fan in cowboy country
We're equally cherished, by the man above
Soon; we'll break bread, 'round a white oak tree

Life is a celebration of all, Eden was created for
It's easy to see; that we're not different at all
Everyone hunts for shells on a rocky shore
All are mesmerized, by a crispy, chilling fall

Denver, New York, Mobile and, Nashville
I have laughed, sung and loved there
Today; I see God's land from a redwood hill
You can see Atlanta; just climb another stair

Come to New Mexico and fold, spicy, fat tacos
Teach us the secrets of creole jambalaya
Sing near the canyons, and hear the echoes
See the faces of the Apache and the Maya

This New Mexico, cowboy; loves you
Dixie's the most beautiful woman, I've ever seen

Mount Rushmore Or Less

Keystone South Dakota, the Black Hills
The great Sioux war of eighteen seventy-six
Affirmation overwhelms, controversy overspills
The answer lies in playing, "pick- up- sticks"

Everything else about the Black Hills, has been a joke
Educate, revoke, feed, revoke demilitarize and revoke
Our brothers listened because they had no choice
English tongues spat words; all they heard, was noise

Confetti treaties written with disappearing ink
Gold, sunbathing above the ground
Black Hills gold! Decaying red bodies stink
King Solomon's mine has been found!

Mount Rushmore or less

"Aint 'nuf room up he'ah for them savages and us"
"They stand and stare; but, they don't say, nothing"
"I don't see, no anger; I don't see no lust for the dust"
"We're taking gold; think we owe them something?"

Dakota land, is our peoples' blood
Faces offour white men on a sacred mountain
In the sky, they're safe from fire and flood
How many moons, until we're free? We're counting

All-righty then! There must be a few laughs in all ofthis
Mount Rushmore or less, less, less
The nitwits spend millions of dollars on their rock of bliss
When their economy and government is a rotting mess

Let's go to Washington and carve a statue of Crazy Horse!
We'll go there with our carving tools; they won't mind
Raised brows and sneers; are just par for the course
After the shock; they'll need some time to unwind

How can these people breath, with all that clothes on?
That man is wearing a black chimney on his head!
They call us, "savages", but; they're the Hun
Let's scare the hell out of them; we'll rise from the dead!

The meek shall inherit the Earth
Let's hang out here and watch them blast each other
In eighteen- sixty-one; they gave Satan a rebirth
White and black against gray; a speckled hen, slaughter

What do we see; that they don't see?
Eyes are all the same, but, they see only red
The mountains and the Earth; are ours for eternity
Yesterday; streams whispered, now; they're dead

The Lakota, Mandan, Chippewa and Sioux:

Let us, in groups of thousands; ride onto their farms
That will be fine; they'll be passive, and let us pillage
They'll allow indiscriminate murder with open arms
We'll hoard them into a lifeless, barren village

Custer and his army:

Major Reno; this territory will suit us, just fine
It's not like those savages can really own anything
I can think of better use for the maple, oak and pine
We'll have them heathens domesticated by spring

Mount Rushmore or less

Did this artist paint an interesting living picture?
Was; madness greed, and godliness; vividly portrayed?
Look around, we're comfortably in the future
Red will forever remain red; this world is in disarray

Mount Rushmore; or less
Mount Rushmore; or less

Milk and Honey

I couldn't get home fast enough
The first day of school in sixty-six
She autographed my right shirt cuff
Green eyes, black hair, what a mix!

My mother's words; remain in my mind
"Not everything that glitters; is gold"
"She's not the best, you'll ever find"
"You'll understand when you grow old"

Milk and Honey

What a utopia; this would be
If every word spoken, led to truth
Not all are born into a life that's free
We don't all get a quarter for a tooth

The land of milk and honey, every day
Any place can be anything you imagine
Homeless and persecuted came to stay
We are history's democratic legend

You must be a realist, before you sail
Prepare; or meet with disappointment
The Channel is restless in gust or gale
Perseverance; is the traveler's ointment

Colonists' milk and honey; popular equality
Let new Americans, salute a flag of freedom
We're known for unwavering hospitality
Send us your hungry; we'll feed them

Homegrown milk and honey; never sour
Irish immigrants in the nineteenth century
Too long; captives in "Big Ben's Tower"
Did they find Ireland, here? You be the referee

Too tired and worn, to keep their homeland
Content to work their fields like me and you
Pittance earnings, for a tax collector's hand
Clans living on turnip and mutton stew

Bees will fight tooth and nail for their honey
Jerseys will kick your butt into a milk can
Orchards didn't sprout, just because of Johnny
We're America; we fought and the others ran

Milk and honey, isn't something you just get
We worked and sacrificed to keep our oasis
Weather didn't stop us: drought, snow or wet
This is a country of Americans, not races

You will be who you want to be, eventually
This pie is large and plentiful; but, hard to cut
We must unite and reach for a slice, mutually
We're a democracy; nothing can crack this nut

If we don't dream; we'll never touch tomorrow
Milk and honey isn't exclusive to free nations
Power in people, overcomes tears and sorrow
The end of the rainbow; marks your destination

This dream, means something different to all of us
We see the Garden of Eden, through different eyes
We need a government that will love us
Unite as a country, before this world dies

Mr. Campbell, Please Sing Us a Song

Most of what's good in this world
Was born in country music
When our lives are in a whirl
We want songs, that'11 heal the sick

New-age country groups are exiting
They sing about love and breaking up
The original masters; are most inviting
We need their magic brew in our cup

Patsy 's, "Crazy", describes us all
Hank's, "Your Cheating Heart", is raw truth
Marty's, "A Pink Carnation", the senior ball
Jim's, "He'll have to go", so very smooth

Mr. Campbell, please sing us a song

Glen, where in the world; are you? In
Wichita, repairing fallen lines? Phoenix
isn 't the place you knew "Southern
Nights", still haunt our minds

People walk away from society every day
We live on a fast-moving slab of granite
Reality comes to us in a different way, but,
We don't sacrifice for success, just to can it

Your voice plays tricks on our soul
We can't wait to see you smiling, as always
You're gone and, we need something to hold
Don't let our memories turn to haze

Mr. Campbell, please sing us a song

I've loved Blue Grass since childhood
Banjos spin me like a storm on a weather vane
I'd reverse the clock by decades, ifI could
Please whisk us back to memory lane

Glen, where in the world; are you? In
Wichita, repairing fallen lines? Phoenix
isn't the same place you knew
Those southern nights, still haunt our minds

"Howdy! I'm, Glen Campbell!"
That's all it took, to get the masses, shouting
''I'm gonna sing 'bout desert sunsets and bramble''
"I'll be singing about the West, this outing"

American icons don't age; they improve
Railroads and role models; keep us going
Without love and brotherhood; we don't move
The people need you, and its showing

We've been waiting for you
Mr. Campbell; please sing us a song
It's dark here; please sing

I remember, when you sang, "back-up"
You belong with the best ofthe legends
We need the classics, fiddles and, "do-wop"
Today's concerts are more like pageants

Glen; it's time to come home
You shake our bones and make us cry
Your six- string topples the Vatican 's dome
No one thrills us like you do; although they try

What more can we say to bring you back?
We love you, Glen

The Blind Boy from Cottonwood Mountain

City people call us bumpkins
They hate us, 'cause, we're not like them
They want law suits; they want injunctions
Things they didn't have that in Bethlehem

There's a blind boy in Cottonwood Mountain
His six-string, makes the angels sing He
cools us like a cold stream fountain We
jig and spin, like toys made of string

Our town's the richest in the state Cottonwood
Mountain; touches the sky Sermons at church
start over, when we're late Our boy, his guitar,
and the moon, gets us high

We were in town last week, chugging through
It looks like a child's painting; if you ask me
Hill folk aint afraid to smile and say, "howdy-do"
We paid a dollar for water; not even that, is free

Music from a park sounded like bobcats in heat
Straining and screeching, electric guitars
I'll take acoustic; with a smooth; and easy beat
They sleep under neon, we sleep with the stars

There's a blind boy on Cottonwood Mountain
He's short on wealth, but, not on love
His first note stops, the sadness and the pouting
He has no money; he depends on the source above

They can have their paper doll kids and glitter
We have different ideas about family
Hearts that don't beat together, become bitter
Tomorrow; they'll see us with clear eyes, finally

In the meantime; we plan for Saturday night,
Our boy wonder from Cottonwood Mountain
We'll be horn piping; everything will be alright
God gave us too many blessings for counting

Fresh, clear, blue grass music!

A blind boy from Cottonwood Mountain!
His fingers move too fast, for watching
He makes the angels, sing, in harmony

Silver City Suits Me Fine

Which side of the Gila did you live in?
Mexicans and Indians on the desert side
The other side is across the ravine
North side shines; let the other side slide

The Murray Hotel, still has swinging doors
Climb up wooden stairs to the sidewalk
Two feet down; tie and water your horse
The saloon inside, is the "Lady Hawk"

Thirty and forty year old cars and trucks
Don't require more than dirt to park
The speed limit is; "Watch out for ducks"
No electric lines; we lived in the dark

Go to school; cross two old bridges
A visit to the greener part of town
Emerald lawns and boxwood hedges
Wasting water, into the ground

Silver City, suits me fine!
Silver City suits me, just, fine!

On our side of town; kids worked too
Shoe-shine boxes made pockets jingle
"Looking good; give me the other shoe"
I did well; I knew where to mingle

North-enders, on their side of the city
They loved our festive celebrations
The decorations were vibrant and pretty
It became one town, on those occasions

Silver City! If it weren't for copper mines
This anthill, would've never been settled
In the twenties, we got telephone lines
It's a town because of ore and metal

Our elders live here, as those before them
Mother Earth was pregnant with silver
Shining eagles, were the state's emblem
So long ago; but the mines still deliver

Cacti and gullies aren't much to brag about
There's no land where we would rather be
I can talk to primrose and rivers out loud
The music in the valleys, is just for me

This sand cake; was an Apache settlement
This is a special place for all people
We have survived drought and embattlement
The Sonoran is ours; ripple by, ripple

Magic! You find it in Saguaros and plateaus
In the Gila River, Taos and Las Cruces
Mellon patches and vineyards; heaven knows
Peaches and oranges; are God 's sunny juices

We make tamales, like no place else
You'11 know you crossed into our state
Aromas from earthen pots, will ring your bells
Tourism is jumping, and our chili 's the bate

What is so enchanting, about Nuevo Mexico?
Ifbeautiful the people don't captivate you;
Get away to "Enchanted Forest" and its snow
The turquois environment, is a witch's brew

Art colonies and the Carlsbad Caverns
Jelly-belly, hot air balloon rides
Eighteen sixties saloons and taverns
Decorations of feathers, pottery and hides

Words of gentle love are written
For the "people's" songs and prose
Dedicated to all those smitten
By the prickly pear and rose

New Mexico, Land ot Enchantment
Yesteryear, today and tomorrow
Experience a river side encampment
Ride! We have horses you can barrow

We'll have hot, red chili waiting for you

Indian giver

There's a pattern to all that breathes
The best of a man, is the strength of his wife
Givers will wear the sacred wreathes
The air is our own; but, we share our life

Do I speak of the weakness of man?
I speak of ignorance that is universal
Why do you pillage from this land?
To take and give back; is just reversal

Native Americans, saw Earth as only theirs'
All people looked the same in their kingdom
We were brothers to Elk, the hawk, and bears
Burning words, were spoken at random

Indian giver! Indian giver!
Words; the color and smell of anger
Use it; but, I cannot give you the river
Our land is dying; from Olympia to Bangor

A gift of the heart is forever and beyond
The love we give today, is eternal Only
clean blood, can form a bond Brotherhood
is freedom, hatred is infernal

Indian giver! Indian giver!

We must banish greed, to save our species
To remain on top of the soil, we must share
 Unending bounty from the flatland and seas
This; for evermore, is every man's fare

Life is perpetual, and there is no fare We saw
the white man, as the holy one Jamestown
survived on, Peoples' fowl and bear We fed
them, until our own food was gone

Fortress gates swung wide, free of locks Red
and white humanity, rippled like a flag We
 taught, how to cook with glowing rocks
They shared tobacco from an elk skin bag

I can give water, and I will give food
Without my arrows and arc, I cross the curtain
The need for my nets and lance, is understood
You can use them until dark; you can be certain

Indian giver! Indian giver!

What is mine, is yours for a while
When the moon is the sun, come to me
We will talk of magnificent things, and smile
I will give you buffalo, you will give me tea

Some things are yours, to keep Some
things, you share with no one Giving; is
holy, mysterious, and deep Return all you
barrow, when work is done

Indian giver! Indian giver!

To lend for a moon; or to keep forever
I cannot give you the heart of my people
Gluttony isolates you, but, fairness is clever
In common land, a king's share, is a ripple

Why can we not journey together?
My eyes see people with thunder sticks
Our arrows fly, but with a feather
Skin of snow and skin of sun, can mix

Victory belongs, not to one who kills most
Power lies in he, who is kin with nature
He will parish those who, dishonor their host
He is mighty; man is a mere creature

The sky and stars belong to us
Ponds, rivers and lakes belong to us
The morning mist; belongs to us
When will understanding, belong to us?

Take my hand, I promise you my world

Westward, Through the Red Lands

Westward through the Red Lands!
Go west, young man; go west!
Don't wony about them Indian bands
Let's put our guns and courage to the test

Independence, is a good place to start The
rush will start from a mile long line Bring
your personals, mules, and a cart
This land is theirs', but, I'll make it mine

The land belongs to whoever gets to it first
Get there fast, and stake it quick
We'll have to survive critters and thirst
We'll find water with a hickory stick

Doing good, making about thirty miles a day
We'll hit the Rockies by autumn at this pace
Trouble; those clouds up ahead are grey
Daddy; that rider has paint on his face!

Westward, through the red lands
Go west, young man; go west!
Don't wony about them Indian bands
We got guns and courage; put 'em to the test

They won't bother us, just curious, that's all
Something's wrong with the last wagon
Was that a coyote howl; or an Indian call?
The dog's looking back; his tail 's not wagging

Must be ten dozen or more on the ridge yonder
If they want something, why don't they say so?
They saw the dead buffalo; it's no wonder
The feathered one's drawing his bow

Let's take a ride through the Red Lands
Nobody lives there, anyhow
Aint nobody owning it

Round them up! Form a circle! Do it quick!
Angry hornets; buzzing arrows in the sky in hundreds
One is buried in my leg! My saddle's getting slick!
Form a barricade; they're cutting us to shreds!

They're leaving, but I don't know why
Started out with eighty five men
The rest of us will, surely die
Forty-three wagons; down to ten

My God! The women; the carnage! The
desert was the color of rawhide
Everything is red, but, the sky is orange
Ride! Enough ofus have died!

Yesterday; the desert was at peace
We held reins of sinew in our hands
Oh, God; help us through this, please
No one told us, these are bad- lands

It'll take all day to bury the dead Don't
know if it 'll get better or worse Any
risk is better than the lives we led We
had a bad day, but it's no curse

Set up guards! Stay awake!
Quiet; like the morning of a first snow fall
Tell the women there's no time to bake
I see a rider on the horizon; dark and tall

Stopped; and he's staring without moving
He plunged his lance into the clay
He's dismounting; what's he proving?
His arms are outstretched, in a peaceful way

The shadow form is growing larger, larger
Twenty feet away, he stops; arms straight out
I'll walk towards him like a fox, not a charger
I can read his face; I know what it's about

"I learned your words in government schools"
"My name is Montgomery; from Lewiston"
"I am Seven Mules"
"Only one man can save you, and, I am the one"

Go back from where you came; and live
Ifl ride onto your land and kill; what will you do?
If you ask and not take and waste, we will give
We fight for home and life; the same as you

Westward through the Red Lands
Go west, young man, go west!
Don't wony 'bout, them, Indian bands
We got guns and courage; put 'em to the test

There's a price to pay for tracking on Indian land
White Eyes; came one day, and were gone the next
Pilgrims come because the reward is grand
Some wear bonnets and rags around their necks

Let's track across the Red Lands
It's not as if a red man, can own anything

The unauthorized, greedy, insurgency continued
Screeching wagons in the thousands trespassed
The massacres were vicious and they were crude
They weren't the first and they weren't the last

Before the "trail of tears"; there was the Red Lands
A dripping carpet of red, runs from here to the sea
Treaty after treaty was torn to strands
Our holy grounds, white villages; will someday be

Our god gave to all; this golden Earth
Someone in anger; painted our homes with blood
No more game; what are the hills and rivers worth?
Humanity, will again suffer the great flood

Our ground is cut by steely wheels
The vulture speaks of what he sees
Our paradise was stolen with forked deals
Everything is lost; yet, we're not on knees

The way of the white man, is the way of taking
Pawnee words; are strong like granite
Tall boots, crossed our land; all forsaking
The Earth is eternal; why can 't all live in it?

Gore and bones cover the floor of our canyons
Our future has flown away with westward winds
This violated ground, does not even grow onions
We live in punishment for the white mans' sins

Westward through the Red Lands
New farms; product of hate and slaughter
Westward through the Red Lands
Gone forever, are the deer, the fish, and otter

You stole our land, Tongues of Snakes
Our sacred land, is now without a soul
You butcher our trees; you plant iron stakes
My son sits and stares at an empty bowl

Who will be first at the gate of pearls?
Who will feel the touch that cleans?
Our people pray as our spirit unfurls
Gods of the soil, have love for all beings

God bless the Red Lands
May they bathe in heavenly tears
God bless the Red Lands
And all who cross these sacred mountains

Someday; all who walk, will be one under the sky
This writing; inspired by: Black Elk, era 1877

Lost In the Black Hills

Jacksonville was brighter than a cop's spotlight
She packed the Pepsi, and I grabbed the Devil Dogs
We were homeward bound, and flying like a kite
I hummed Hank Williams, while she sawed logs

I'm proud of being a fourth generation trucker
Sitting behind the wheel, is as natural as breathing
Signs whiz by: White River, Belvidere and Tucker
I'm done in, and my backside's taking a beating

I think highway forty's, around route sixteen
There should've been a sign, twelve miles back
Pine forests everywhere; it looks like a magazine
I'm way off course; I need to get on track

Ifwe're lost; I'm real glad it's here
I see a glow on the horizon! We need sleep
A hot meal, warm bed, and some ice-cold beer
Let's call it a night; the road's too steep

Miss; what state are we in?
"You're in the Bad Lands ofthe Lakota"
"You're in the Western Rockies region"
"Sixty miles from Keystone, South Dakota"

You didn't tell us the name of this town
"The elders call it "Spirit Falls"
"Why are all the trees and grass, brown?"
"Things die, when the counsel calls"

Am I crazy? I can see you there; tray in hand I
see the kitchen without looking around you
"Gold buttons, cut us down, and took our land"
"Every ten years; we visit the land we knew"

Lost in the Black Hills of South Dakota

"Don't be afraid; the food we give to you is real"
"Someday all souls, will bind in brotherhood"
"We were glad to share; they didn't have to steal"
"What Earth gives, is for all; that's understood"

"Go, now; and you will be there in four hours"
"You will not lose your way again"
The clouds are bright; they look like ivory towers
How do we explain what just happened?

I can't remember the last time I felt this alive
Let's keep this miracle ride to ourselves
Things won't be the same when we arrive
The tavern took me back to unicorns and elves

We were lost in the Dakota Black Hills

A Championship Buckle

My leg was already busted
When the gate sprang open
Too quick; I didn't get adjusted
I was pulling, I was groping

Cracked my leg the week before
Lost my leg, but not my spirit
Said it was sprained; nothing more
A young bull; I couldn't steer it

A championship buckle
All cowboys' heart and soul
A championship buckle
A rider's Super Bowl

Without cut hands and sacrifice
Life is, wood ponies on shiny springs
After eight seconds; comes paradise
We spit blood, for what it brings

I scream alone, into the night
A year ago, someone shared my pain
My head spins; so does my sight
Busting at my age, is insane

I do what free Americans do
Nothing matters but self- respect
The man in heaven, pulls me through
All macho brawn; short on intellect

A Championship buckle
My family drove away

Circuit winners are buckets ofbones
They have admirers by the dozen
Shiny trucks, but don't pay the loans
New boots, but their assets are frozen

When I can't ride any more,
I'll recall the days of youth and sun
Tomorrow, I'll knock on her door
My second life's just begun